TWAYNE'S WORLD AUTHORS SERIES
A Survey of the World's Literature

Sylvia E. Bowman, Indiana University
GENERAL EDITOR

SPAIN

Gerald Wade, Vanderbilt University
EDITOR

Jacinto Benavente

(TWAS 57)

TWAYNE'S WORLD AUTHORS SERIES (TWAS)

The purpose of TWAS is to survey the major writers —novelists, dramatists, historians, poets, philosophers, and critics—of the nations of the world. Among the national literatures covered are those of Australia, Canada, China, Eastern Europe, France, Germany, Greece, India, Italy, Japan, Latin America, New Zealand, Poland, Russia, Scandinavia, Spain, and the African nations, as well as Hebrew, Yiddish, and Latin Classical literatures. This survey is complemented by Twayne's United States Authors Series and English Authors Series

The intent of each volume in these series is to present a critical-analytical study of the works of the writer; to include biographical and historical material that may be necessary for understanding, appreciation, and critical appraisal of the writer; and to present all material in clear, concise English—but not to vitiate the scholarly content of the work by doing so.

Jacinto Benavente

By MARCELINO C. PEÑUELAS

University of Washington

Translated by Kay Engler

Twayne Publishers, Inc.   ::   New York

Library of Congress Catalog Card Number: 68–9515

Preface

Jacinto Benavente was the most popular Spanish playwright of the first half of the twentieth century. His prestige extended throughout the world and he won the Nobel Prize for Literature in 1922. Nevertheless, the worth of his dramatic works has been much discussed. The studies which have been published about them often point out their virtues and criticize their defects from very general and less than objective points of view. His plays have been praised or condemned with far too much emotion.

Today, now that the first centennial of his birth (he was born in 1866) is just past, and with the advantage of a certain perspective, one can make of Benavente's abundant dramatic production a critical study that is free from fleeting impressions and emotions, and thus place it in the position it justly deserves. That is the major purpose of this book.

I have tried to place Benavente, the man and the writer, in the age in which he lived; to study his relationship with the Spanish and European theater of his time; and to analyze the similarities and differences between Benavente and the other writers of his and later generations. I have attempted to discover what Benavente's work meant at the beginning of the century and what it means today in the Spanish and European theater. Through detailed analysis of his most representative plays, and through considerations of a more general nature, I shall try to point out the positive and negative qualities of his theater; to study the nature of his themes and techniques; to make a classification of his plays and to outline the philosophical, moral and ideological position which, implicitly or explicitly, the author takes in his plays.

M. P.

Contents

Chronology

1866   August 12: Benavente is born in Madrid.

1871–   Primary and secondary school. Constructs toy theaters
1882   and writes little plays which he acts out with his friends.

1882   Enrolls in the University of Madrid. Unenthusiastically begins to study law.

1885   His father dies. He abandons his studies and dedicates himself to reading and writing.

1892   He publishes his first work, *Teatro fantástico (Fantasy Plays)*.[1]

1893   *Versos (Poems)*, a book of poetry, and *Cartas de mujeres (Letters from Women)*.

1894   October 6: Première of his first play, *El nido ajeno (The Intruder)*.

1896   October 21: First theatrical success, *Gente conocida (Well-Known People)*.

1899   Edits the journal *Vida literaria (Literary life)*.

1901   October 8: *La gobernadora (The Governor's Wife)*. He had already produced 19 of his plays.

1903   March 17: *La noche del sábado (The Witches' Sabbath)*.

1905   December 1: *Los malhechores del bien (The Evildoers of Good)*.

1907   December 9: *Los intereses creados (The Bonds of Interest)*. He had now produced 53 plays.

1908   February 22: *Señora ama (The Lady of the House)*.

1909   Founds the "Teatro de los niños" ("Children's Theater") and premières, on December 20, *El príncipe que todo lo aprendió de los libros (The Prince Who Learned Everything from Books)* and *Ganarse la vida (To Earn a Living)*.

1908–   He writes a few plays, but dedicates himself primarily
1912   to journalism. Publishes weekly articles in *El Imparcial (The Impartial)*.

1912 He is elected to the Spanish Royal Academy. As he never became an active member, the Academy, in 1946, named him an honorary member.

1913 December 12: *La malquerida (The Ill-Beloved)*.

1922 Receives the Nobel Prize for literature. At this time he had already premièred some one hundred plays. Travels through Latin America and the United States.

1920– No play of his is presented in Spain, as he is upset by
1924 the attitude of some critics. Declares that he will not write any more for the theater.

1924 February 24: He is granted the Great Cross of Alfonso el Sabio. The Madrid City Council names him Favorite Son of the city.

1924 In the face of these tributes, he ignores his previous declaration and on April 2, premières *Lecciones de buen amor (Lessons in Good Love)*.

1928 November 21: *Pepa Doncel*.

1929 Travels several months in Russia. He is named president of the *Montepío* (Pension Fund for Widows and Orphans) of the Union of Authors.

1936– The years of the Civil War. He spends them in Val-
1939 encia without premièring any plays.

1944 Fifty years have passed since the première of his first play. Tributes to Benavente are offered all over Spain and his most famous plays are produced.

1945 January 19: *Nieve en mayo (Snow in May)*. He had now premièred 150 plays.

1945 July 20: At the head of a theatrical company, he sets out for Argentina. During the trip he reaches the age of 79.

1945 December 6: Première, in Buenos Aires, of *La Infanzona (The Noblewoman)*.

1948 In April, he is awarded the "Mariano de Cavia Prize" for the best newspaper article published in the Spanish press during the previous year.

1954 July 14: Dies in Madrid at the age of 88. In this same year he premièred three plays: *Hijos, padres de sus padres (The Sons Are as Fathers)* on February 11; *El marido de bronce (A Husband in Bronze)* on April 23; and *Por salvar su amor (To Save his Love)* on November 2. In his long life he had written and staged 172 plays.

CHAPTER 1

Some Facts About the Life and Personality of Benavente

BENAVENTE'S childhood was spent in an atmosphere that encouraged his strong inclination toward the theater. He was the youngest of three children. His father, Mariano Benavente, the son of a modest family, studied medicine amidst great poverty. He soon gained a solid reputation as a pediatrician. He was director of the Hospital of the Child Jesus, a member of the Royal Academy of Medicine, an outstanding author of scientific articles, and a man of much learning. In 1866 a bust in his honor was erected in the Retiro Park in Madrid.

The Benavente house was full of books of all kinds. "In my father's library," says Benavente, "works on medicine alternated with literary works. I have read from both since I was very young. Only when I was in high school and exams were approaching would he attempt to hide some novel . . ."[1]

As a very young child he read with an interest far beyond his years, even, as he tells us, to the point of memorizing selections from the works of great Spanish and foreign dramatists. He was also fond of the melodramatic novels of Manuel Fernández y González and of Enrique Pérez Escrich, and of adventure stories.

His father's clientele was made up of the best of Madrid society of the period, aristocratic families as well as writers and artists. Benavente himself says of it: "José Echegaray was a client of my father since the period in which he [Echegaray] was a minister in the cabinet of Amadeo de Saboya. Many were the mornings when he would appear at our house very early to take my father in his carriage, before he visited the *Inclusa* (foundling home) to see his very young son, a delicate child who was his father's greatest worry."[2] Other friends and clients of Mariano Benavente were Juan Valera, who had two children; certain important politicians (Bravo Murillo, Práxedes Mateo Sagasta, Francisco Silvela, Francisco Romero Robledo); and artists of the theater (Antonio Vico, Calvo, Emilio Mario and María Tubau).

In this atmosphere there soon arose in Benavente a great enthusiasm for literature, particularly for drama. He was a precocious child: "Predestined by that great passion of my life which reading has been, I learned to read without realizing it, with little difficulty or effort on my part, and with only a few lessons from my brothers and my love of books. In view of such a fortunate disposition, my father decided that I might go to the *colegio*."[3]

Nevertheless he did not like the *colegio*, a municipal school near his house, even though he did have an affectionate memory of his first teacher:

My passion for reading and the ease with which I learned whatever I heard or read does not mean that I had any love for studying; I never have had, because of the subjection to order and discipline which studying implies. I learned as I would play, by a free expansion of my intelligence. I never willingly went to the *colegio* . . . My schoolmates were almost all sons of modest merchants of the neighborhood: a son of the coal merchant on our street; the children of a wool merchant and mattress maker who had his establishment on the ground floor of our house; a son of a tavernkeeper on the same street, all very well behaved and very neat. It was neither they nor the teacher who displeased me, but the school itself, only because it was a school. The same thing has happened to me with all *colegios*, and in the university it became a real phobia. The only good memory I have of my school years is of vacations and of playing hooky . . .[4]

His contact with the theater and theatrical productions began very soon, even before he had reached the age of four. Speaking of his "initiation as a spectator," he tells us that "I was very young, so young that I still had a nurse; with her and my family I went to the theater, the Variety Theater which was near our house." He recalls that it was a fantasy, *Juanilla la de Jerez (Juanilla, The Girl from Jerez)*. "I suppose," he says, "that it was a play from the seventeenth or the beginning of the eighteenth century, probably by Diamante." He went to sleep, and about the play itself remembers only a "monstruous dragon's head spewing fire from its eyes and mouth," and that they took him home before the performance had ended. He adds: "Certainly afterwards there was no play, comedy or musical which I attended in those years from 1870 to 1878 that I didn't remember vividly."[5] At this time he was between four and twelve years old.

He also tells us of his attendance, at about the same time, at the performance of the first few of Echegaray's plays, "from *La esposa del vengador (The Revenger's Wife)* to *En el seno de la muerte (In the Heart of Death),* from which I learned, when the copy dedicated to my father arrived at our house, whole passages which I have not yet forgotten."[6]

On another occasion, Benavente speaks of the performance, in 1881, of *El gran galeoto (The Great Galeoto),* when he was fifteen: "I went with one of my brothers, a great admirer of Echegaray, as I, too, was and always have been."[7]

At this time he was, in his own words, a child "more reserved than outgoing, and somewhat given to meditation." He read a great deal, books of all kinds: "My first reading of *Hamlet,*" he wrote in 1949, "was in a translation by Moratín; later I read it again in the French translation by the son of Victor Hugo, and at last, when I was about sixteen, I was able to read it in English."[8] Between the ages of twelve and sixteen he had learned French, English, Italian, and some Latin.

His interest in the theater was not only as a reader and spectator. Since his early childhood he had also been an actor and writer. His first toys were little chapels and altars. Benavente, playing with other children, would often deliver sermons to them, even though, as he tells us, he did not particularly enjoy going to mass. "This sacred oratory was the first manifestation of my literary interests . . . (but) I soon put aside my habit. Priestly vestments, altars and saints were soon retired to a corner among worn-out toys. From then on little theaters were my only toys."[9]

With his young friends he had what he calls an "avant-garde theater . . . an ideal theater, with no audience," where they staged battles and duels, improvising the dialogue. Later, they gave performances before the neighbors. He speaks with pride and emotion of these memories:

My toys! My theater! The stage, backdrops, wires, costumes, bright colors, puppets . . . I was the only actor. My voice was then capable of imitating any voice. I mimicked the actors and actresses then in vogue, both Spaniards and foreigners; and with the greatest admiration from adults, I recited on my own and in a natural voice scenes and fragments in verse from many different plays, both ancient and modern. . . . And my audience, an audience of maids and youngsters, understood the greatest works of all time and of all the theaters of the world. Shakespeare, Schiller, Molière, Lope de Vega, Calderón, Tirso, Rojas, Alarcón, Moreto, and all the romantic theater . . . The maids even memorized the lines.[10]

He also speaks of the first play he wrote:

My first work was written, of course, for my theater. It was a fairy tale in one act: *El gato pardo (The Leopard)*. My brother Mario liked it so well that he thought it worthy of a larger stage (he tried to sell it to a puppet show, but they only offered him seven and a half pesetas instead of the twelve and a half which he asked, so he didn't sell it) . . . Afterwards, like a good producer, I wrote a spectacle, *Los cazadores de leones (The Lion Hunters)*, to take advantage of some delightful lions which someone had given me. I never bought toys nor asked to be given toys which couldn't be used in my theater. I also wrote a really great spectacle, in thirty or forty scenes, in imitation of one which had been given at the Chatelet Theater in Paris with the same title, *Las mil y una noches (A Thousand and One Nights)* . . . It was never produced, as it was the year in which I graduated from high school (I must have been about sixteen). It seemed to my father that I was not studying as much as I should, so he soon suspended the performances. I gave the theater away so that I would no longer see it quiet and sad. That was my farewell to childhoood. The day I stopped being a child on the outside; within, I continued my life of imagination. I would be an actor, or I would be nothing. From that day on I was very withdrawn. I communicated my thoughts to no one. I lived only my inner life and was always sad, very sad. I had never thought of being an author, but an actor, yes, it had been the great illusion of my life. It was the only possible escape . . .[11]

Even when he had become famous as a dramatist he continued

[16]

to repeat, as he had always done, his desire to be an actor in the theater rather than a writer.

During these years he was as attracted to the circus as to the theater. When the season began in Madrid he would go every Sunday afternoon. So great was his affection for the circus that it was never in all his life diminished. He especially loved the clowns, always referring to them with the English word "clown." The life of the circus is reflected in such plays as *La fuerza bruta (Brute Force)* and *Los cachorros (The Cubs)*. Some critics— Cejador and Walter Starkie, among others—have even mantained that he was the manager of a circus which visited Russia, but this is only a legend which Benavente himself has denied.

Having put aside his little toy theater and now graduated from high school, he entered the university. His father wanted him to be an engineer, but he did not like mathematics and spent a difficult period while studying it. He then began to study law, but never finished his studies:

Of the three years I spent at the university I have no better memories than of the days I was absent, cutting classes, and of some great friendships with intelligent fellows . . . The days we cut class offered us the opportunity to know Madrid like the back of our hands in our wanderings about the city. Its lower-class neighborhoods, its suburbs, even its cemeteries . . . The professors should have been grateful for our absence, for when we did attend class it was only to cause a disturbance and demoralize the others . . .[12]

He was in the third year of his studies, quite tired of university discipline, when his father died. He was then nineteen. As his mother allowed him to do as he pleased, he soon abandoned his studies, and as he later said, he was never sorry for having done so. He then dedicated himself to reading a great deal of his own and to traveling in several European countries, particularly between 1885 and 1892. His father had left the family with sufficient financial resources so that Jacinto was able to dedicate himself fully and with no worries to his career as a writer. He could thus afford to wait until his works were accepted, and the high point of his career arrived without his facing economic problems.

At that time he was living a life typical of a wealthy young man of Madrid, getting up late, traveling, playing chess, attending the society parties and *tertulias** of that time, and reading and writing at leisure. Sáinz de Robles describes him in that period in the following terms:

> Jacinto was a very well-dressed young man, almost a fashion plate, with the appearance of money and smoothness of speech and manner, so his presence was received with somewhat condescending affection. Before traveling through France and Italy he had, for a long time, been quite adept at dividing his time among aristocratic salons, diplomatic receptions, the dull affairs of the *petite bourgeoisie*, Bohemian coffee houses and the library of the literary society. At that time he had grown a small beard and his hair was getting thin . . . he began the leisurely enjoyment of some gigantic Havana cigars . . .[13]

Angel Lázaro, years later, about 1898, when Benavente had become a famous playwright, paints a similar portrait:

> His small figure; dark, sharply-featured face; prematurely bald head; long curled mustache; black, pointed beard and enormous cigar—the cigar with which Benavente is always pictured in photographs and caricatures and without which he would no longer be recognizable—are familiar sights in the Café de Madrid, were Valle-Inclán, Rubén Darío, Luis Bello, Pío Baroja, Ricardo Baroja, Martínez Sierra and other persons such as an occasional comic or some student interested in literature formed the inevitable *tertulia*.[14]

Around 1890, before he had yet become known as an author, he worked successfully as an actor in the company of María Tubau, a famous artist of that period. Some time later he organized a theatrical company and toured several provinces accompanied by "the beautiful Geraldine," an actress and circus artist. It was said that Benavente was in love with her, something which he always denied even though he wrote poetry in her honor and the memory of her remained with him for many years.

All his life he enjoyed being on stage, and often acted out parts in his own plays. He frequently recited the prologue to *Los intereses creados (The Bonds of Interest)* and repeatedly

---

* Translator's note: A *tertulia* is a social gathering of a group of people who customarily meet for the purpose of conversation.

played the role of Crispín. Responding to a reporter's question about what he might have liked to be, he answered, "An actor. It is my true calling. Writing for the theater has only been an extension of my love for the theater."[15] The beginning of his career as a dramatist was not easy. Benavente himself tells of the performance of his first work, *El nido ajeno (The Intruder)*, in 1894, when he was twenty-eight:

I had presented ten or twelve plays to Don Emilio Mario (a friend of the family and manager of the Teatro de la Comedia) before he would accept any one of them even as a bad play. This went on for six or seven years. The first play was poorly received by the public, and its reception by the critics was even worse, so that to produce the second play I had to overcome even greater obstacles. And, of course, this second one, *Gente conocida*. (Well-known People), was written long before the first one.[16]

Before he became known as a playwright he had published three books: *Teatro Fantástico (Fantasy Plays)*, 1892, eight short dramatic pieces, in dialogue, based on dreams and fantasies which had always attracted him; a book of poetry, *Versos (Poems)*, in 1893; and in the same year, *Cartas de mujeres (Letters from Women)*.

He was also interested in journalism. In 1895 he wrote his first article for *La Epoca*. He was later director of *Vida literaria* and *Madrid cómico*. He also collaborated on *Revista contemporánea, La Ilustración española, El arte del teatro, La lectura, Helios, Alma española* and *El Imparcial*. He worked alternately on his journalistic articles and on his plays because, as he said, he tired of writing for a deadline. His journalistic works, published in his *Obras completas (Complete Works)*, fill 1578 pages. As he was also a distinguished lecturer, 312 pages of his lectures are included in the same collection. He would often write in bed and liked to retire late, almost always after three in the morning. He also read, took his breakfast, and even ate and received visitors while in bed. He loved to visit the theaters, chatting with the famous artists in their dressing rooms and telling jokes and shocking stories with delight.

He was superstitious and never denied it. He tells of the peculiar circumstances surrounding the death of his father, who died while reading Shakespeare's *King Lear*. The book subsequently came into his own hands. Later, when a publishing house asked him to translate one of Shakespeare's plays, he chose that very one. He adds: "Chance is the explanation which ignorance always gives to whatever it doesn't understand, as does wisdom itself when it is afraid of understanding too much. I have never believed in chance, for this reason I have always been very superstitious. Coincidences frighten me."[17] He also liked to repeat the following curious facts about the date of Shakespeare's birth in 1564: "Add up the numbers: one and five, six; six and six, twelve; twelve and four, sixteen. Well, the year of his death was 1616, the sum of the numbers in his birth date written twice. Undoubtedly a coincidence, but he himself said, in the words of Hamlet: 'There are more things in heaven and earth, Horatio, than are dreamt of in your philosophy.'" He repeated this in writing on various occasions.

He was voluble and inconsistent in his opinions and statements. He flitted about from one political position to another. He also said several times that he would not write anymore for the theater. One of those who customarily attended the *tertulia* in the Café Lisboa, Gonzalo Latorre, held an interview with him which appeared in *La Acción* (May 13, 1921), and in which he declared:

I'm not going to write any more plays, with the exception of the one I have promised to the great American actress Una O'Neill and which will be produced in English.
"Are you serious, don Jacinto?"
"Indeed, I am."
Later the reporter returned to the same question:
"But is it true what you said before?"
"Absolutely true."
"May I ask the reason for your decision?"
"Well, I can live more quietly that way."
"Then, you will write no more?"
"Perhaps a novel, I don't know; but as for the theater, as long as I can live without it I will never again put a single word on paper."[18]

At that time he was upset by the attacks of some critics. A short time later, in 1922, he went to South America as the director of the acting company of the Argentine actress Lola Membrives. During the trip he was awarded the Nobel Prize. With all the honors and acclamations he forgot his promise to retire.

He wrote a great deal about himself, his ideas, attitudes, and temperament, but he wrote very little about his private life, as did few other Spanish writers. He left his *Recuerdos y olvidos: Memorias (Things Remembered and Forgotten: Memoirs)* unedited and unfinished, but they were published by Aguilar in 1962. In them he comments on the lack of memoirs, autobiographies, diaries, or private confessions in Spanish literature:

At first glance it may appear the result of great modesty. The Spaniard has never been much given to undressing in public, physically or spiritually. Is it, then, modesty or excessive pride? It clearly is not modesty a very Spanish quality; it is, rather, haughtiness or pride which often manifests itself in the fear of ridicule, something about which perhaps no other people are so sensitive as the Spanish. This often leads us to appear more ridiculous . . . [19]

His *Memoirs*, too, contain very little about his private life. Only concerning his childhood does he relate the very personal details that demonstrate his prodigious memory. The rest consists of memories, anecdotes and facts about people he knew, friends or neighbors, actors and aristocrats, impressions of the Madrid of his time, etc.

His plan, as he himself tells us, was to divide his *Memoirs* into three parts: the first, from 1866 to 1886; the second, from 1886 until the end of the nineteenth century; and the last, "as far as I go into the twentieth century." He began to write them during the civil war, in 1937, under circumstances which were hardly conducive to reminiscence and serene reflection. The first part comprises 428 pages; the second, only twenty-three. They end abruptly, perhaps because of circumstances resulting from the civil war. Unfortuntely he never wrote, as was his intention, the very important part concerning his literary career and his relationships with the public, actors and critics. In any event, the *Memoirs* are interesting in that they make known some important facets of his personality.

Like any great artist, he was conceited and very sensitive to criticism. He was always flattered at the sight of his name on the show billboards. It was because of this, and because he had to make his living from the theater that he wrote so much, indeed, too much. He was voluble and unpredictable, and there was always a marked difference between what he said and what he ultimately did.

But it is his work which interests us, and in it there are consistency, unity, a clear line of artistic development. He put Spanish life of a half a century on stage, as he saw it. His cold satire is saturated with a fine irony which is always very much his own, unique, very "Benaventine." Clearly, he occupies one of the most important positions in the history of the Spanish theater.

CHAPTER 2

Benavente, Reformer of the Spanish Theater

THE première of Benavente's first play, *The Intruder,* in 1894, signaled the appearance of a new technique, a new sensibility, on the Spanish stage. The traditional practices of the Golden Age dramatists had changed very little until the end of the nineteenth century. The traditional theater was dominated by the action which took place on stage, by poetic recitation and the gestures of the actors, all done in an emphatic manner. Benavente introduced naturalness of speech and action. It was a step appropriate to the reformation of the drama and to the beginning of modern theater in Spain.

Nevertheless there had been precedents in the European theater and in the Spanish theater as well. Benavente incorporated these precedents into his work by giving concrete form to the new currents which had appeared in the second half of the nineteenth century. The new sensibility, the new attitude of reform, was indeed reflected in all Spanish literature as expressed in many varied forms by those writers who were members of the Generation of 1898. (See following chapter.)

Also, there had been remote antecedents in the eighteenth century, in the plays of Leandro Fernández Moratín which were later destroyed in part by the Romantic theater. The immediate forerunners were the playwrights of nineteenth-century realism.

I   *Forerunners of Benavente in the Spanish*
Theater of the Nineteenth Century

During the first half of the nineteenth century, in contrast to the Romantic fever, there were several writers who maintained the tradition of realism. Nevertheless, influenced by the inescapable atmosphere, they began writing plays in the Romantic vein. But at the same time, they reacted against the excess of the theater of the age and produced distinctive plays in the *costumbrista** tradition, following the pattern laid down by Moratín and Ramón de la Cruz in the eighteenth century.

Although in many cases the intrinsic value of their plays is not great, it may be helpful to remember some of these writers for the important part they played in keeping alive a Spanish tradition which had temporarily been suffocated by the fever of Romanticism.

As early as 1818, *La indulgencia para todos (Indulgence for All)* by Manuel Eduardo Gorostiza (1789-1851), a writer born in Mexico but who was educated and lived in Spain for many years, was performed. In this play Gorostiza follows the style of Moratín in presenting sober portraits of contemporary life. Together with plays in the Romantic style, he wrote others, like *Contigo pan y cebolla (Bread, Onions and You)*, 1833, in which he parodies the emotional exaggeration of the drama typical of that period. A disciple of Zorrilla, Narciso Serra (1830-1877), also wrote Romantic plays and comedies of manners, as did playwrights like Francisco Flores Arenas and Tomás Rodríguez Rubí. All are writers now of little importance.

Together with them, one should remember the most popular writer of comedy of that period, Manuel Bretón de los Herreros (1796-1873). A man who wrote easily, he produced more than a hundred plays. He was particularly good at satirical comedies like *A Madrid me vuelvo (I'm Going Back to Madrid)*, 1828, full of caricaturesque exaggerations, with rapid, lively dialogue in a distinctly popular vein, and at parodies of the extreme of Romanticism, like *Muérete y verás (Die and You'll See)*, 1837. In some details he is reminiscent of Moratín, although the tone is always more popular and the accent is clearly on comedy. In many of his portrayals of the life of the time he approached the *costumbrista* style of Ramón de la Cruz.

---

* Translator's note: *Costumbrismo* was a literary tendency of the last century, involving the portrayal of the daily life and prevailing customs of a particular region or level of society. (*Costumbrista*—one who wrote literary works in this style; also used as adjective, referring to this style.)

Of greater artistic and human value are the plays of those dramatists who midway through the nineteenth century turned toward the so-called "high comedy," which followed the tradition of realism with moral intent and which was opposed to the Romantic style of the period. The performance, in 1845, of *El hombre de mundo (The Man of the World)*, by Ventura de la Vega (1807-1865), was a significant step in this new direction. Born in Argentina, he was a poet clearly superior to his predecessors, although not now considered among the best. The play just mentioned (his best) clearly aims at naturalness on stage. The spirit and form of his *costumbrista* plays indicate the style he would impose on his later works: simplicity and swiftness of action, naturalness and spontaneity in the development of the plot conflict and in the dialogue, a psychological treatment of character and even a bit of frivolity in contrast to the solemn and melodramatic Romantics. Ventura de la Vega is an obvious forerunner of Benavente in his dramatic style.

The same may be said of Ventura de la Vega's disciple, Adelardo López de Ayala (1828-1879), famous in his time as a politician as well as a writer. His first plays were written in Romantic style, although there could already be noted in them a tendency toward sobriety and an absence of exaggerated idealism. In 1857, he opened *El tejado de vidrio (The Glass Roof)*, in which he launched a well-aimed attack on the vices and faults of society, from then on employing the tradition of "high comedy" of contemporary manners and mores. It is a carefully written play showing great attention to detail; a work of great naturalness with truth and irony in the treatment of characters and situations, and careful observation of contemporary reality. The same qualities are evident in *El tanto por ciento (The Percentage)*, 1861, *El nuevo don Juan (The New Don Juan)*, 1863, and *Consuelo* (1878), his most successful work.

The comedies of manners form only a part (not the most important) of the work of Manuel Tamayo y Baus (1829-1898). They should be remembered here because they fit into the tradition of realism and into the *costumbrismo* of some writers of the period who reacted against the excess of the Romantics. After opening several different plays—a tragedy, *Virginia* (1853); an historical play, *La rica hembra (The Rich Female)*, 1854;

and a psychological play, *Locura de amor (The Madness of Love)*, 1855, his first work in prose—he wrote a comedy of manners, *La bola de nieve (The Snowball)*, 1856, on the problems and consequences of jealousy. This was followed by *Lo positivo (The Positive)*, 1862, inspired by a French play, and by *Lances de honor (The Duels)*, 1863, a thesis play in which he attacked the contemporary attitude toward dueling. In these plays he continues to simplify the action and seeks the most direct and concise expression by reducing the number of characters and using prose. Tamayo's masterpiece, *Un drama nuevo (A New Play)*, 1867, is not a *costumbrista* play. It concerns characters from Shakespeare's dramas, and even the English author himself appears on stage. It is an excellent play, one of the best of the past century, and offers the innovation of the "play within a play" which Pirandello later developed in a masterly fashion with the appearance on stage of the author and even the prompter.

Continuing the "realist" movement of the nineteenth century with surer steps and more modern emphasis was Enrique Gaspar (1842-1902), a writer who unfortunately is little known today. Since the première of his first drama, a work in prose, *Las Circunstancias (The Circumstances)*, 1867, he clearly and conscientiously defined his dramatic theory, divorcing himself from both the Romantic and the traditional Spanish theater. He had previously written a dozen minor works in verse. In all he wrote some fifty plays in as many years of a theatrical career spread over the second half of the nineteenth century.

In *Circumstances* he introduces the man in the street, a character very different from the exalted heroes of that period; he employs spontaneity of action and gesture; and fabricates a natural, brief and concise dialogue on incidents of daily life. In short, he presents naturalness and spontaneity rather than theatricality and exaggeration.

In addition to these exterior or formal characteristics, there is in Gaspar's work a new thematic orientation which clashed with the conventions accepted at that time by the public and the theatrical impresarios. The five characters of *Circumstances* act in a manner which is neither exemplary nor virtuous, motivated always by purely monetary interests. They act only out of self-interest when circumstances are favorable to them, something which occurs continually throughout the work. There is one incident—of a young girl seduced and left in a state of desperation by her seducer—which did not seem particularly edifying to the theatrical censor. Gaspar was forced to change the play by adding a new scene, thus making the ending false and conventional, but in agreement with the taste of the public. The seducer, in a scene which changes completely the moral intention of the incident, publicly redeems himself by promising to marry the young girl.

Gaspar's second prose work, *La levita (The Frock Coat)*, 1868, is a harsh satire on middle-class vanity. After a few other plays of minor importance, he opened, in 1890, *Las personas decentes (Decent People)*, the best play he wrote. It is a social satire in the form of unconnected scenes, very similar to Benavente's *Well-known People*. The objects of his satire are those seemingly decent people who live in a world of hypocrisy and deceit. The dialogue is rapid, lively and clever. There are no love scenes, signs of sentimentality nor theatrical effects.

Gaspar conscientiously adhered to certain clearly defined dramatic principles which were precursors of Benavente's theater in theme and technique. He was decidedly opposed to the tradition of Echegaray's theater. He knew well and admired the French theater of his time; his drama was, in part, inspired by it. He was well aware of the need for a reformation in the Spanish theater and of the revolutionary orientation of his work, although he was also aware of the difficulties of the undertaking, as he said: "Nothing is more dangerous . . . than to break with a tradition, especially so glorious a tradition as that of our own theater; but the evolutionary process goes on and there is no way to turn back. For some time now the public has forseen it; today it demands it; the difficulty lies in its accepting the new delicacy when it still retains a taste for its traditional food."[1]

Among Spanish dramatists, Gaspar particularly admired Manuel Tamayo y Baus and Adelardo López de Ayala; among French dramatists, Emilio Augier, Dumas Fils and Sardou. His theories about the production and staging of plays, expressed in *Problemas (Problems)*, a play written in 1877 and performed in 1882, and in *Soledad* (*Solitude*)—a novel published in 1877 based on the play *La resurrección de Lázaro* (*The Resurrection of Lazarus*), first performed in 1878—coincide with those of the revolutionary French theater of that period, with Le Théâtre Libre, which was begun in Paris in 1877 and which will be discussed later in this chapter.

Enrique Gaspar's relatively obscure position today is in part due to the fact that his innovations, so contrary to the public's tastes, were neutralized by the opposing, neo-Romantic current represented by Echegaray, who, with his noisy success, came to dominate the Spanish theater of the end of the century. The public had never understood Gaspar's plays, and the producers, who usually consider the theater solely a business, rejected them. He was also disadvantaged by the fact that he lived a great part of his life abroad as consul in France, Greece and China. But as the initiator of the trend toward modernity in the Spanish theater he deserves a more important place. "Without exaggerating a bit," says Daniel Poyán Díaz, the author of the best published study on Gaspar, "it can be said that there is no other writer in all the years of the second half of the last century who serves as a clearer antecedent, a more adequate explanation for the understanding of the evolution of our theater."[2]

II *Benavente and Echegaray*

In the last third of the nineteenth century the theater of José Echegaray (1832-1916) apeared as an anachronistic parenthesis in the revolutionary process begun by the writers just discussed. It meant turning backward along the road that led from Enrique Gaspar to Benavente. Technically and thematically, Echegaray's theater looks toward the past, toward the Romantic and Calderonian tradition. Nevertheless, Echegaray was very popular in his time, among both Spanish and foreign public. He was awarded the Nobel Prize in 1905 and his most famous play, *The Great Galeoto* (1881), was performed with great success throughout Europe.

After the later triumphs of the new theater with its naturalness and spontaneity, so different from Echegaray's melodramatic affectation and grandiloquent verse, the critics have regarded his work with disdain. It is unjust to forget that there is a great deal that is good in Echegaray's theater. Along with its defects, there are many genuine virtues: vigor and forcefulness, psychological depth, and exceptional mastery of technique and structure.

Echegaray's first period is characterized by artificiality and grandiloquence carried to the extreme. As Angel Valbuena Prat wrote, "Echegaray's extensive work is . . . abundant and uneven . . . his theater is an amalgam of genius and eccentricity."[3] The exaggeration of passion, sentiment and gesture becomes excessive. The very titles of his first plays are indicative of this spirit: *La esposa del vengador (The Revenger's Wife)*, 1874, *En el puño de la espada (On the Hilt of the Sword)*, 1875, *En el pilar y en la cruz (On the Pillar and the Cross)*, 1878, *En el sueño de la muerte (In the Dream of Death)*, 1879. Afterward, although the defects did not disappear, Echegary wrote plays with touches of dramatic forcefulness and creative genius which reached their peak in *The Great Galeoto*. After 1890, he wrote dramas of a very different tone. He even composed plays of light but polished satire like *Un crítico incipiente, (A Would-Be Critic)*, 1891, and *Mariana* (1892) in a style which, especially in the dialogue, approaches that of Benavente's works. Although in the last-named play the ending preserves the clearly Romantic spirit of his theater, other plays even reflect some of the style of Ibsen.

Some Spanish playwrights of that period imitated Echegaray's manner, probably influenced by the great success which his works had enjoyed. Among them were Leopoldo Cano, Eugenio Sellés, Angel Guimerá, Joaquín Dicenta and Ceferino Palencia; but none of them reached the level of their master.

Benavente's theater has been considered by critics and public alike to be the antithesis of Echegaray's. Quite rightly so, for nothing is more diametrically opposed than the style, the spirit, of the works of both authors. Nevertheless, Benavente deeply admired Echegaray. In a letter written in 1932 he wrote: "My admiration for don José Echegaray? I wouldn't know how to explain it; it is something closely allied to the best memories of my childhood and youth . . . For me he has been, and is, the best Spanish dramatist of the nineteenth century . . . No

Spanish writer has influenced me so much."[4] It seems certain that Benavente, in this categorical affirmation, is referring to the influence which Echegaray had on him in his childhood and early youth when he had attended a performance of Echegaray's plays, which always made a great impression on his sensitive spirit. He would often memorize passages which he later recited with pleasure for Echegaray himself, a friend and client of his father, as well as for other people. Perhaps this early admiration helped to awaken in him the desire to be a playwright.

On the other hand, as Ismael Sánchez Etevan, in his biographical study of Benavente, recalls, twenty years earlier, in 1912, Benavente had answered journalist-critic González Fiol, better known by his pseudonym, "El Bachiller Corchuelo": "What writers have influenced you?" "Galdós." "Do you really think that Galdós is our best dramatist?" "Yes."[5]

In one of his articles, "De sobremesa" ("Table Talk"), Benavente again tells of his admiration for Galdós: "All who know me, all who have heard me, know how great is my admiration for him whom I have always claimed as master. I learned to write plays from his novels rather than from the foreign models which many think have influenced me."[6] There is no doubt that the admiration which he felt for Echegaray was due above all to sentimental reasons, to childhood memories. Yet, it was also in part due to his recognition of the indubitable technical mastery which is evident in Echegaray's work.

Benavente's theater is closer to that of Galdós. There are, however, important differences between them, as much in the general spirit of the work as in their attitudes toward social problems, clearly revolutionary in Galdós and conservative in Benavente.

III   Benavente and Galdós

The dramatic work of Benito Pérez Galdós (1843-1920) thus takes on particular significance in any discussion of the immediate precedents of Benavente's theater. Galdós, like Gaspar, realized the necessity of a reformation of the drama leading toward naturalness and spontaneity. In an article in 1885, nine years before the première of Benavente's *The Intruder,* he wrote: "In order for the theater to set foot firmly in the school of realism, it is necessary for a forceful writer to begin the march and undertake this great reform as best he can." He was mistaken in pointing to Echegaray as the writer he thought could best carry out the reform, although he realized the difficulties involved, adding: "Echegaray, who possesses the greatest ability imaginable, is the one to lead the way. He needs only to clip his wings a little, to fly a little lower, and to concern himself more with the true expression of human feelings than with effects obtained through exceptional conflicts . . ."[7] Clearly Galdós was asking a lot of Echegaray, nothing less than ceasing to be himself as a dramatist.

In another article he shows the same preoccupation which was already worrying other writers: "The fact that the theater is in a state of decadence is something that's beginning to smell like a sick man's stew, so much has been said and written about it. The public is tired of the old forms of the drama, it knows them from memory, it knows the tricks as well as the best writers, and is hardly attracted by the plays which for years have been its delight."[8]

Galdós is here surely confusing the public's taste with his own and with that of a small group of writers preoccupied with the necessary renovation, for the man in the street does not like change. Innovators must always confront the accepted tradition, the preferences and habits of the public as a whole. There were signs, however, that a change was imminent. It is possible that Galdós himself attempted the reform, and, carried away by his uncertainty and worry, began to write for the theater. He presented his first play, *Realidad (Reality),* in 1892, published previously as a novel, in 1889.

Galdós began his dramatic career after twenty years of writing novels. He was, above all, a novelist by vocation and temperament, but with a definite inclination toward drama. From the beginning he had written novels in dialogue form, like *Reality* itself. Nevertheless, he never succeeded in mastering the technique of the theater as he had mastered novelistic technique. He lacked a sense of synthesis in the action, ability to present characters and atmosphere on stage, and a sense of proportion in dialogue. In his plays there is always more drama than theater, more dramatic conflict than technique.

At the same time, he brought to the theater thematic elements—social and religious problems—which broadened the possibilities of the theater of his time. What is more important, he brought to the stage a new style, a new spirit which was completely different, at times completely opposed, to the traditional theater. His work was oriented toward an authentic revolution, a formal and thematic reformation of the Spanish theater.

Reality, for example, presents a new attitude toward conjugal honor which is completely different from the traditional attitude. The protagonist, in the end, even pardons his unfaithful wife. The play produced violent reactions of displeasure from the public and of indifference or misunderstanding from some critics who found it ". . . not only slow and heavy, because of its novelistic flavor, but too psychological for the masses and offensive to general taste."9 It also produced enthusiasm in small sectors of the public.

Nevertheless, Galdós was not the first Spanish dramatist who portrayed on stage understanding and pardon instead of the solution of violent revenge to which the Spanish public had become accustomed since the sixteenth century. In 1870 we find the same spirit in *Los hombres de bien (Men of Good Will)* by Manuel Tamayo y Baus; and a year before the première of *Reality*, in *Un libro viejo (An Old Book)* by José Feliu y Codina.

In his next play, *La loca de la casa (The Mad Woman of the House)*, first presented in 1893—also adapted from a novel, and technically better than *Reality*—Galdós succeeded in interesting both public and critics in the problems presented: the conflict between a strong and pugnacious man of the street who has become rich through his own efforts, and an educated, refined woman from high society who marries him in order to solve her bankrupt family's economic problem. Among the twenty-two plays which Galdós wrote, it is one of the best. Another of his plays on the same artistic level is *El abuelo (The Grandfather)*, also adapted from a novel in 1904.

The plays by Galdós which were most successful with the public are not exactly his best: *La de San Quintín (The Lady from San Quintin)*, a sociological play (the love affairs of a duchess and a socialist worker), and *Electra* (1901), in which Galdós again deals with the religious theme which he had used in several novels: *Doña Perfecta, La familia de Leon Roch (Leon Roch's family), Nazarín.* The performance of these two works awoke great popular enthusiasm, particularly because of their themes and also because of the use of theatrical conventions and concessions to the public. In both cases popular demonstrations of support were organized and the people accompanied him home with great acclaim.

Galdós was an authentic revolutionary in the Spanish theater. He brought to the stage a courageous and honest realism full of understanding and humanity, of modern preoccupation with social problems. It was a theater which signaled a reaction against things Romantic, particularly against the Romanticism of Echegaray with its passionate and melodramatic explosions. It raised Spanish theater, thematically, to the level of European theater. Galdós' drama represents a link between that of Enrique Gaspar and that of Benavente. Yet, he went much further than either in his frank portrayal of social conflicts. Galdós was a revolutionary who looked to the future, to the betterment of Spain. Benavente, ideologically, was a conservative, indifferent to the deep conflicts within Spanish society.

Nevertheless, Benavente's theater also meant a reaction against the anachronistic, turn-of-the-century Romanticism of Echegaray. Against a background of the affected gesture, the hollow voice, the melodramatic, declamatory and solemn tone, the violence of passion and the traditional concept of honor, appeared the theater of clever conversation in a confidential, ironic and satirical tone which Benavente succeeded in popularizing. Thus Benavente breaks definitively with the old tradition which had reigned in the theater of Spain since Lope de Vega in the seventeenth century. Yet at no time does his work cease to be Spanish. As one who knew the new European trends well, he assimilated technique and spirit, incorporating them in the national context.

Die-hard Spanish traditionalists have always rejected foreign influences, considering them negative and harmful, contrary to the Spanish spirit. "Can anyone who denies and breaks with traditional continuity truly be a model for new generations?"[10] wonders Vila Selma (referring to Benavente), worried by the loss of certain aspects of the old tradition.

The question must be answered with an emphatic yes, precisely because Benavente lays to one side certain antiquated attitudes which are far removed from the mentality of the modern world, both in and outside of Spain. This does not imply that whatever is authentically Spanish must be disowned. Benavente never does this. One has only to recall his unconditional admiration for Calderón and for Lope de Vega, whom he rates above Shakespeare as a dramatist (a case in which he is evidently carried too far by his enthusiasm). "For me," Benavente has said, "Lope de Vega is superior to Shakespeare [and the] greatest work of our theater is Calderón's *La vida es sueño (Life Is a Dream)*. This does not keep me from believing that Lope de Vega is, on the whole, superior to Calderón. One play is not an author, nor an author one play."[11]

Benavente, always very Spanish, could not disown the artistic tradition of his country. Nor could he disown certain aspects of its historical and cultural past. He disowned only some old attitudes—a social and human concept of honor, the narrowness and rigidity of false religious views, grandiloquence and melodrama, theatricality of gesture—all of which he rightly considered to be extinct in the dramatic art of his time.

IV *Benavente and the Foreign Theater*

The remarks just quoted about Lope and Shakespeare were expressed by Benavente in the course of an interview with a journalist. On such occasions, the enthusiasm of the moment often made him say more than he had intended.

Benavente knew Shakespeare's work very well. He had read and studied it. He continually quoted from it, in articles, lectures and conversations. The English playwright was his idol, his guide. The admiration which he felt for him can only be compared to his admiration for Cervantes. He intended to translate all of Shakespeare's plays, and promised this to the publishing house, "La lectura," who even announced the forth-coming translation. Undoubtedly for lack of time and for the constant pressure of producing his plays, he never completed the task. He only translated or adapted a few comedies and *King Lear*.

In an article, "April of Destiny" ("Abril predestinado"),[12] he speaks emotionally of his deep admiration for the English writer in warm and tender words. He speaks of his visit to Shakespeare's native city, Stratford-on-Avon, of the church where his remains lie, of the city and its residents. The article is a dovoted homage to the master.

In the prologue to *Cuento de amor (A Tale of Love)*, an adaptation of Shakespeare's play *Twelfth Night or What You Will*, he says in the words of the Countess Olivia: "I am the prologue to a tale of love, which happened where all tales happen, in the enchanted realm of the poets . . . A divine poet, a demigod, he knew how to weave a tale with mysterious simplicity, and that immortal spirit which lit the whole world, penetrated hell and touched heaven . . . Protected by the divine poet . . . a humble poet of this time asks admiration for Shakespeare in all that is admirable and for himself all criticism."[13]

All of this has led some critics to want to find traces of Shakespeare in Benavente's plays. Walter Starkie, for example, even says: "There is a touch of the sublime coldness of Shakespeare in Benavente which allows him on occasion to climb to the summit and to contemplate humanity. His spirit has many of the qualities associated with the classic . . ."[14]

Statements like this which rate Benavente's work so highly often go too far; they clearly lack a sense of proportion. Gonzalo Torrente Ballester puts the question in the proper perspective: "It is often said that Benavente counts Shakespeare among his immediate predecessors; it is one of the most incomprehensive statements ever made, with no other actual basis probably, than the affection and admiration of the Spanish playwright for the English playwright, and his vanity in admitting as his such an illustrious ancestor. There is nothing more opposed than their respective temperaments: if Shakespeare is essentially a poet, Benavente never even touches the world of poetry. If we restrict the claim to the purely formal, even to the purely technical, the differences are so great and so fundamental that they do not warrant establishing any relationship between the techniques of one and the other."[15]

There does not appear to be any trace in Benavente of Shakespeare or of any other foreign—or Spanish—writer prior to the nineteenth century, with the exception of Molière (whose Don Juan play he translated) and Leandro Fernández de Moratín. With the latter, however, there is only a slight resemblance, a coincidence in their satirical attitude. There is no direct influence.

As for Henrik Ibsen (1828-1906), certain reminiscences of this playwright's work appear in Benavente, although more in form than in attitude. Perhaps the marginal similarity to the Northern playwright is due to the fact that Ibsen's dramatic methods spread throughout the European theater of the second half of the nineteenth century and reached Benavente through French dramatists.

Later, at the beginning of our century, Benavente wrote a study on Ibsen that appeared in the first issue of the *Revista ibérica (Iberian Review)* of July 20, 1902. At that time Benavente had already produced twenty-three of his plays (including translations of the Molière Don Juan play in 1897, and of *Libertad (Freedom)* by the Catalan, Santiago Rusiñol, in 1902). He had already written his most important plays, *The Intruder* (1894), *Well-Known People* (1896), *La comida de las fieras (Food for Wild Beasts)*, 1898, *Lo cursi (The Thing to Do)*, 1901, *La gobernadora (The Governor's Wife)*, 1901. It is possible, however, that he had long since been familiar with Ibsen's work. If there were something of Ibsen in Benavente's plays, it was because there was something of Ibsen in almost all European dramatists of that period. In the "self-critique" which Benavente published in the newspaper *La Información (Information)* on his second play, *Well-Known People*, the day following its première (October 21, 1896), there is a significant commentary:

If there is some moral ideal at the bottom of this play it is this. The aristocracy of ability, of talent, the political aristocracy, shall we say, makes fun of and plays with the aristocracies of family and wealth, exploiting them as it wishes; but over the aristocracy of the individual, over the woman who is alone, but strong, the only alert mind among all those sleeping minds, it has no power. Now you see that by digging a little, some traces of Ibsen can be found in my plays; but I must confess that this was not my intention and that only now do I understand that my play may be thought of in this way . . .[16]

The immediate precedents for Benavente's dramatic formula must be sought among the French playwrights of the end of the nineteenth century. They were writers characterized, like Benavente, by the rather cynicism with which they satirized contemporary French society, whether the bourgeoisie or the upper classes. These writers treated the theme of love with such freedom and frankness that their plays appeared too daring, even immoral, especially to audiences with a Puritan tradition like that in the United States at the turn of the century.

This new French theater gained impetus with the revolution begun by Le Théâtre Libre, founded in 1887, and carried on by the personal vigor of André Antoine, who was later, at the beginning of this century, to become the famous director of the Théâtre Odéon of Paris. Antoine, among other innovations, revolutionized traditional methods of staging and directing. He introduced naturalness on stage with reforms which were daring in his time, such as that of actors speaking with their backs to the audience. He also produced Ibsen's plays for the first time in France. At the same time, his efforts went toward producing the revolutionary plays of young playwrights which no one accepted because they clashed with the prejudices and habits of the theater managements and of the public.

The tendencies of the new aesthetics prompted by Antoine, summed up by Adolphe Thalasso in his work *The Free Theater*,[17] are of interest in that they show certain characteristics which are later reflected in Benavente's plays. The new dramatic theory is oriented toward simplicity of action in contrast to heavy, complicated plots. Again, the study of reality and the creation of more natural characters replace pure intrigue. Furthermore, the author seeks conciseness and swiftness of movement; good, solid characters are eliminated; the writers seek the "morality" of their plays in the life which surrounds them, with the result that this morality often seems "immoral"; the theater must be a reflection of life as it is, not as we wish it to be. These revolutionary writers consider it normal that in their plays the guilty and the innocent alike are hurt.

There is, nevertheless, one characteristic of this new theater which Benavente seldom follows and which, when he does follow it in some of his plays, becomes a defect: the facts alone should explain the play; in other words, there should not be "explicators" who comment upon, explain and justify the action. In many of Benavente's plays, *La ciudad alegre y confiada (The Happy and Confident City), La propia estimación (Self-Esteem), Nieve en mayo (Snow in May), Divorcio de almas (A Divorce of Souls), La ciudad doliente (The Sorrowful City), Su amante esposa (His Loving Wife),* etc., there is an abundance of dialectical speeches in which the author's attitude is too transparent, a fault which Benavente himself recognized. He lets himself be carried away by his didacticism and, through the characters, expresses ideas which have little or nothing to do with the action of the play.

Among the French writers of the new wave of the Théâtre Libre there are three whose plays Benavente knew and which should have significantly influenced his style and technique:

1) Alfred Capus (1858-1922), with his light, entertaining comedies which are always an ironical satire of contemporary French society. They are well-constructed plays of polished prose, like *La Veine (The Vein)* and *Les deux écoles (Two₁ Schools),* a free yet comic satire on divorce, in which the author portrays interesting bourgeois types and worldly women of life in Paris; or *Le petit fonctionnaire (The little Bureaucrat),* a criticism of provincial life. Capus is a *costumbrista* who, like Benavente in many of his plays, does not go beyond the superficial in the problems he treats. He also frequently includes aristocratic characters, as in *Le Prince d'Aurec (The Prince of Aurec).*

2) Maurice Donnay (1859-1945), who usually deals with the theme of love in a light, cynical style, with touches of sentimentality. He does not fail to criticize the life of the bourgeoisie of his time. His best play, *Amants (Lovers),* brings together his most typical qualities.

3) Henry Lavedan (1859-1940), who portrays French customs at the turn of the century with moralistic overtones. An uneven

writer, like Benavente, he also began his theatrical career with short dialogues which he published in newspapers. His first play, *Une famille (A Family)*, is very similar to many of Benavente's in its detailed observations, excellent dialogue and satirical intent. The same can be said of his *Nouveau Jeu (A New Game)*.

Other playwrights of the same generation who may have influenced Benavente, although probably to a lesser extent, are Countess Martel, François de Curel, Eugène Brieux, Paul Hervieu, Jules Lemaitre and Henri Bataille.

Benavente was aware that in his first plays, particularly in *Well-Known People*, the style is similar to that of the French writers just mentioned. In the "self-critique" already cited which he published in the newspaper *Information*, printed as a prologue to *Well-Known People*, he says: "The composition of last night's play is one used by several well-known writers: Lavedan and Countess Martel, among others. One may perhaps find the greatest similarity between last night's play and the works of the latter, greater than with Father Coloma's *Pequeñeces (Trivialities)* or Gaspar's *Decent People*."[18]

Because of all this Benavente has been accused of not being Spanish, of incorporating into the theater of Spain at the end of the nineteenth and the beginning of the twentieth century a manner, technique and spirit foreign to everything typically Spanish. "Perhaps without his knowing it," says Vila Selma, "he is more foreign than Spanish. Whatever is new in Benavente's theater is something which singularly sets itself apart from the traditional course."[19] Benavente is undoubtedly a cosmopolitan writer and he introduced into Spain, together with other playwrights, attitudes and ideas which indeed clashed with the traditional ones. But they were currents and tendencies which had been floating through the European air of the last century and which would inevitably have come to Spain. They were part of the eternal restlessness of young writers who are always seeking new forms of expression to reflect the sensibility of the time. They were, in this case, following the general course laid down by Ibsen.

But Benavente, in spite of his formal and thematic innovations, continued to be very Spanish. His theater faithfully reflects certain aspects of Spanish life of his time. His spirit is as Spanish as that of Lope, for example, even though there is a difference of three centuries. Azorín says it best: "Benavente himself cites French predecessors to his theater in the prologue to one of his plays. Benavente was only half right. The foreign likeness is only skin deep; the substance of Benaventine theater, even in the beginning, is totally Spanish."[20]

Andrés González Blanco also rejects the idea that Benavente's theater is lacking in Spanish spirit. Commenting upon the innovations which Benavente introduced, coinciding with those of the French writers of his time, he rejects the idea of imitation or plagiarism from the French theater: "There was no such imitation and even less plagiarism . . . There was instead a reformation of the Spanish theater."[21]

This is all quite evident. The character types, situations, atmosphere, the characters' mentality, the morality implicit in Benavente's work are all authentically Spanish from beginning to end. The technique, the attitude or sensibility in the treatment of human problems, was undoubtedly something new, but something which was being incorporated into Spanish life as in the rest of Europe with the passage of time. To attempt to go on maintaining the traditional attitudes would have been an effort both futile and anachronistic, as well as meaningless. The new, once again, inevitably replaced the old. Although the public at first showed some displeasure and a lack of understanding, more because of the change in dramatic technique than because of the spirit of the work, Benavente's innovative formula had soon established itself. People began to react agreeably to the new sensibility, even though in the beginning, almost out of habit, it failed to accept the innovation publicly.

For this reason, the opposition to, or rather the lack of understanding of Benavente's first plays on the part of one sector of the critics and the public was much more superficial than what has often been said in critical studies and literary textbooks. There were protests and some attacks against the new practices, but Benavente's success came quickly and easily. The "battle" which Benavente had to carry on with his turn-of-the-century audience has been greatly exaggerated. After the performance of his second play, *Well-Known People*, which was very successful with the critics and the public alike, he was soon recognized as an important writer. He had won the battle beforehand. The atmosphere of life in Spain of that period was perfectly prepared to receive his work. With his innovations Spanish theater was raised to the highest level of European theater.

Nevertheless, Benavente's work is somewhat short of strength and energy. It is a "bland" theater. His apparently daring satires and attacks are always softened by his fear of disrupting too much, of offending the public, by his timidity in the face of serious problems. It is an affable, conservative theater in essence, although at first glance it does not seem so, with its gay, clever dialogues of ironical, yet at times melancholic, frivolity.

Benavente's characters do not live through deep conflicts. They speak of small problems of daily life, always within a concrete, defined social context. This is all part of a superficial, skeptical view of life. Benavente is never preoccupied, in his plays, with human problems in a wider philosophical and social context. They are individualized problems, problems of the individual alone in contact or confrontation with social conventions. "The benaventine character," says Vila Selma, "finds the purpose of his short life within and for himself. He does not live by illusion or hope . . . the life which excites the character is of interest only to himself."[22]

In Benavente's work there is little preoccupation with the meaning of life or with the beyond; the preoccupation is, rather, with the here and now. The complexities of the characters' inner lives are not expressed artistically in a religious view of life, or in the oppressive uncertainty of existential anguish. The work's possible transcendence appears only indirectly or marginally. It is a meaning rooted in the skeptical, ironically pessimistic view of life which Benavente often expressed. Only occasionally does he seem to have faith in "love" as a last resource. I say "seem" because not even then does Benavente convince us that he truly believes in love except as a facile solution to the conflicts presented in the play: a conventional resolution which the undemanding audience always willingly accepted.

Benavente's characters live within themselves, defending themselves from others, shielding themselves against the curiosity, maliciousness or evil of those who surround them. It seems that the author sees hypocrisy as an essential characteristic of man, hypocrisy which is motivated by the impossibility of authentic human communication and which obligates man to withdraw within himself, in a constant attitude of defense. All this is gilded with sentimental touches, with an eye toward the tastes of Benavente's self-satisfied middle-class audience, who only in this way could accept the bitter pill which he presented to it.

This explains Benavente's continued success for half a century. His popularity was limited to an audience of the comfortable middle class, the satisfied bourgeoisie who had no serious social or economic worries. It was an audience whom Benavente always aimed to please and whom he placated with occasional shows of shrewd daring; this, because he didn't face up to the problems with a certain indignation, no one took seriously.

Consequently, the Benavente who was a reformer in the turn-of-the-century Spanish theater, who so influenced that theater with his innovations, cut himself short. There is nothing in him of the authentic revolutionary. In his plays he ably disguises his bourgeoise conformity with the appearance of harsh and revolutionary criticism. It should be made clear that his reform was more formal, or technical, than thematic, although there is also in it the expression of a new sensibility, clearly focused on naturalness on stage. But here he stopped. He never came to experience the artistic and human anxieties which appeared at the turn of the century in Europe and in Spain with the writers of the Generation of '98. Some of these writers, like Valle-Inclán and Unamuno, were true revolutionaries, although they were only marginally interested in drama.

At the beginning of this century there were two trends in the Spanish theater: that of Benavente and his followers, which was the one which prevailed on the stage, and that of the attempts at drama by some writers of '98 (particularly Valle-Inclán), who with their artistic restlessness were at the front of the new European movements.

V Followers of Benavente

Those who continued Benavente's practices, with little of their leader's talent, copied only the most superficial elements and never really grasped the new directions. That is to say, the

Benaventine school of drama, based on new European attitudes of the end of the last century, soon left the road of reform. It had stopped halfway. Although it grew out of a revolutionary principle, it stagnated soon after it was begun, became conservative in form and content, and divorced itself from the new trends in the European and Spanish theater in whose evolution Benavente had, in the beginning, played so great a part. It remained static in the face of the opening of new pathways, particularly after the outbreak of the war in 1914.

Among the important followers of Benavente is Manuel Linares Rivas (1867-1938). He employs some of Benavente's themes, with an inclination toward thesis plays of a moral tone, attacking so-called "good society." He, too, never gets to the root of the problems, exposing only the consequences of the conventions of established customs, backed up by old judicial structures and by the attitude of the Church. He advocates divorce in *Aire de afuera (Spirit from Without)*, 1903, and later in the play which made him famous, *La garra (The Claw)*, 1914, in which the life of a man, married and divorced in America, is destroyed by the "claw" of the indissolubility of marriage in the eyes of the Church when he marries for the second time in Spain and his first marriage is discovered. Rivas harshly criticized the aristocracy in *La estirpe de Júpiter (The Lineage of Jupiter)*, 1904, and in *Cobardías (Cowardice)*, 1919. In *Fantasmas (Ghosts)*, 1915, he attacked old prejudices about conjugal honor. In *El abolengo (The Lineage)*, 1904, one of his best plays, he examines the incompatibility of a married couple: a frivolous woman too worried about her lineage and her husband, a wealthy middle-class man with a different origin and upbringing.

The technique of these plays, oriented always toward naturalness and spontaneity, is impeccable; plot development is very clear; dialogues are clever and ironic, like those of Benavente. A faithful follower of Benavente's theater, Rivas was nevertheless no mere imitator. Within the Benaventine school he does have a distinct personality.

Linares Rivas' plays have a certain vigor, a quality which is missing in another of Benavente's followers, Gregorio Martínez Sierra (1881-1947), whose plays were very successful in the theater and many of which were later made into movies. His popularity among wide sectors of the middle-class public is due to the saccharine tone which impregnates his plays, to the slightly optimistic note of human kindness, and to a bland cordiality which seeks poetic qualities and which often results in sentimentality. The action is always simple, tending to avoid the tragic. As with Benavente, feminine characters occupy the center of his plays. But Martínez Sierra's women are too uncomplicated to seem authentic. His reality has only one dimension.

His most famous play *Canción de cuna (Cradle Song)*, 1911 had great success in England and in the United States, where it has more than once been presented on television. The action takes place in a convent at whose door is left one day a new-born baby girl who grows up among the nuns until she leaves the convent to be married. This play brings together the major characteristics of Martínez Sierra's theater, carrying sweetness, optimism, kindness and sentimentality touching on "corniness" to an extreme. The same thing happens in other plays like *Primavera en otoño (Springtime in Autumn)*, 1911, and *Mamá* (1912), both in the *costumbrista* tradition, and in *El reino de Dios (The Kingdom of God)*, 1915.

Playwrights of the same school, also very popular, were the brothers Serafín (1871-1938) and Joaquín (1873-1944) Álvarez Quintero, who together wrote almost a hundred plays. The majority are *sainetes** and *costumbrista* plays about life in Andalucía. Theirs is an unpretentious, low-keyed theater of superficial *costumbrismo* whose sole purpose is to please and entertain an undemanding audience. It is saved, in part, by its charm and humor, a certain psychological subtlety, the lightness of its themes, and its popular realism. In trying to please the public, the Quinteros, like Martínez Sierra, frequently fall into a kind of facile sentimentality in plays intended to be more serious, like *Malva loca (Loco Weed)*, 1912, *La rima eterna (Eternal Rhyme)*, 1910, and *Las flores (The Flowers)*, 1901, which is perhaps their best work. They at times hit their mark in light plays in a comic vein, such as *La buena sombra (The Good Shade)*, 1898, a

---

* Translator's note: *Sainete is* a short dramatic sketch, usually of only one act; its tone is light and it is most often of a popular nature. Originally it was often presented at the end of a full-length play.

musical comedy, and *El genio alegre (The Merry Disposition)*, 1906. Although they present the people and atmosphere of Andalucía with a certain charm, the theater of the Quinteros never approaches the level of greatness. It is only fairly good.

Together with these dramatists one might also mention others of lesser importance who followed the road laid out by Benavente. But this theater, which, as we have seen, promised a reformation at the end of the last century, limited itself by remaining along the margin of the new artistic and ideological restlessness which appeared at that time with the writers of the Generation of '98, into which group Benavente's attitude toward reform may be placed only with great reservations. That is, Benavente and his followers soon withdrew themselves from the evolution of the European and Spanish theater with which they had, at the beginning, some affinity. For this reason, although Benavente undoubtedly influenced twentieth-century Spanish writers, the best of his followers oriented their works in other directions and Benavente's theater was soon out of date. It soon became old and today holds little interest for the Spanish people.

VI *New Spanish Drama at the Beginning of the Twentieth Century*

One of the most original writers of the beginning of this century, a contemporary of the Generation of '98 although not really a part of it, is Jacinto Grau (1877-1958). He rebelled against the commercialization of the theater, against what he called "industrial theater," and wrote without paying much attention to the tastes of the public. He is inclined toward an intellectual theater which is symbolic and psychologically penetrating. His first important play *Entre llamas (In Flames)*, 1905, demonstrated his artistic independence. He used themes from medieval Spanish ballads in *El conde Alarcos (Count Alarcos)*, 1917, from the Bible in *El hijo pródigo (The Prodigal Son)*, 1918, and also touched on the Don Juan myth in his *Don Juan de Carillana (Don Juan of Carillana)*, 1913, and in *El burlador que no se burla (The Joker Who Doesn't Joke)*, which was never performed.

A very independent writer with a strong personality, Grau occupies a unique place among those who explored new directions in the Spanish theater at the beginning of this century. A restless spirit, he himself expressed his artistic philosophy thus: "To be sensitive to the opposite and to flee from all systems, has been, and is, for me, the greatest goal." This is said in the prologue to the edition of his plays, *The Prodigal Son* and *El señor de Pigmalión (Pygmalion)*[23] which the author considers the peak of his creative effort.

In my opinion, the best play he wrote is *Pygmalion*, a daring work which the author calls a "tragicomic farce," in which some puppets built by a modern Pygmalion end up having more reality than their creator, and in the end, destroying him. This play anticipates Pirandello and can be considered among the best plays of twentieth-century European theater. The play is, perhaps, prophetic, and has exceptional significance today. The puppets, complex machines with a life of their own, which Pygmalion cannot control and which often rebel against him, may be the computers and modern devices of destruction which we are both proud and fearful of having created, not knowing where they are taking us.

Jacinto Grau's theater, full of a tension that is intellectualized and contrary to the taste of the masses, was too new for the Spanish stage. Martínez Sierra, one of the most powerful impresarios of that period, rejected his plays. Nevertheless, Grau was translated into several languages and was well liked abroad.

Some writers of the Generation of '98 also wrote for the theater, although only marginally. They, too, cultivated a dramatic art completely different from that which was popular at the time, the theater of Benavente, Martínez Sierra and the Quintero brothers. It was, rather, a theater which sought new roads and which could never please the mass audience which prefer undiluted, conventional entertainment.

Angel Ganivet and Antonio Machado, together with his brother Manuel, wrote a few plays of little importance. Plays occupy a more important, although still secondary, place in the work of Miguel de Unamuno (1864-1936). He modernized classic myths in *Fedra (Phaedra)*, 1910, and in *Medea*. In *Sombras de sueño (Dream-Shadows)*, 1920, *El otro (The Other)*, 1926, and in *El hermano Juan (Brother John)*, 1929, there are reflections of the same metaphysical problems which Unamuno presents in his essays, poetry, and novels: an existential anguish which searches for the meaning of life and death, speculating on the nature of reality. His plays tend to do away with realism on stage, something which had reigned in the European theater since Ibsen. His theater is metaphysical, yet does not employ symbolism. There is no social motivation nor preoccupation with psychological analysis. Yet, throughout, the ideas expressed are always superior to their dramatic realization, for he lacked mastery of dramatic technique.

In the Generation of '98 there are authentic efforts at reform in the plays of Azorín and of Valle-Inclán. Juan Martínez Ruíz (1876-1967), better known by his pseudonym "Azorín," wrote very original plays in a surrealistic vein, fusing a world of dreams, mystery and hallucination with the real and literary world, in which he rebels against the realism of the turn of the century. They are "Chamber" dramas, written for the minority, difficult to perform, like *Old Spain* and *Brandy, mucho Brandy (Brandy, Lots of Brandy)*. Among the best are *Doctor Death, de tres a cinco (Doctor Death, from Three to Five)*, a short play, one of three published under the title of *Lo Invisible (The Invisible)*, and *Angelita*, on the theme of time, with which he was so preoccupied. Above all an essayist, Azorín never completely mastered the technique of drama.

The most original and interesting playwright of the Generation of '98 is Ramón del Valle-Inclán (1870-1936), with his tragic farce, *Retablo de la avaricia, la lujuria y la muerte (A Tableau of Avarice, Lust and Death)*; his "barbaric" plays, *Romance de lobos (Romance of the Wolves)* and *Cara de plata (Silver Face)*; and the creation of an original view of drama, in violent distortions of characters and situations which he called *esperpentos* (horrible or hideous things, implying an element of absurdity), as in *The Cuckold Don Friolera*, a grotesque and tragic parody on the traditional concept of honor. His theater, like Unamuno's, is anti-bourgeois, anti-Ibsen, and makes little use of psychology. With it he was far ahead of his time, preceding literary and dramatic movements which would appear later and which are much in vogue in today's European "theater of the absurd."

The theater which came after the Generation of '98 continued along new paths, with the poetic orientation of Federico García Lorca (1898-1936) and of Alejandro Casona (1903-1965). After the Spanish Civil War (1936-1939), the Spanish theater has taken two very different roads: one of purely comic entertainment, or one of very serious theater which is completely "committed" to the problems of contemporary man. With these new currents, Benavente's theater is today quite forgotten by the Spanish public.

It is not strange that Benavente's plays arouse little interest today. The theater is that art form which can most quickly go out of date. Almost no play written in prose has survived its own time, its own generation. Only the poetic theater lives on, and not for solely theatrical reasons. The dramatic work is usually too closely linked to the circumstances of the moment in which it appears, particularly if its tone is *costumbrista,* as is the tone of most of Benavente's plays. With the exception of plays set outside of time and space, like *The Bonds of Interest* or *La noche del sábado (The Witches' Sabbath),* his theater has been "surpassed" by that of other writers more attuned to the times. The same thing has happened and will continue to happen to other outstanding playwrights, Spanish and foreign.

CHAPTER 3

Benavente Between the Generation of 1898 and Modernism

THE difficulties which arise out of any attempt to define rigidly such literary concepts as "Generation of '98"[1] and "Modernism"[2] are only too evident when one tries to fit writers like Benavente into one of them. The numerous studies published on both literary movements too often insist on a definitive categorization of writers into one group or another. Apart from the fact that the very basis for the formation of groups of writers by generations, although generally accepted, is rather questionable, ("There are now as many reasons for accepting the existence of the Generation of '98 as there are for denying it," says Rafael Ferreres),[3] the problem becomes even more complicated in the case of the Generation of '98 and Modernism, for they were contemporary movements which, although different in orientation, are fused in the works of many writers.

As Dámaso Alonso wrote, "Modernism and the Generation of '98 are heterogeneous concepts . . . Modernism above all is a technique; the position of the Generation of '98, let us say it in German for more clarity, is a *Weltanschunng*, a world view, . . . the two concepts are not comparable . . . they are not mutually exclusive, but may often be mixed together or combined in a single poet or even in a single poem."[4] Hence the attempt to establish a rigid classification of writers for the purpose of clarity also introduces, in this case, certain elements of confusion. The results of the categorizations which have been made so far speak for themselves. There are no two exactly the same and Benavente is included in the Generation of '98 in some, and among the Modernists in others.

Among the most famous commentators is Azorín, who created the concept of the Generation of 1898, and who includes in the group Valle-Inclán, *Benavente*, Pío Baroja, Manuel Bueno, Ramiro de Maeztu, Miguel de Unamuno, Rubén Darío, and himself. There is also Pedro Salinas, who mentions only the most outstanding in each group: Generation of 1898, Unamuno, Azorín, Baroja and Antonio Machado; Modernism, Rubén Darío, Manuel Machado and Juan Ramón Jiménez. Pedro Laín Entralgo includes in the Generation of '98: Unamuno, Ganivet, Azorín, Baroja, Antonio Machado, Valle-Inclán, Maeztu, *Benavente*, Juan Ramón Jiménez, Manuel Bueno, and a few others. Hans Jeschke places Unamuno, Ganivet, *Benavente*, Valle-Inclán, Baroja, Azorín and Antonio Machado in the same group. Guillermo Díaz Plaja considers Modernism opposed to the Generation of '98, grouping the writers in the following manner, including the dates of their birth: Generation of '98, Unamuno (1864), Ganivet (1865), Baroja (1872), Azorín (1873), Maeztu (1874), Antonio Machado (1876); Modernists, *Benavente* (1866), Darío (1867), Valle-Inclán (1869), Manuel Machado (1874), Villaespesa (1877), Marquina (1879), Juan Ramón Jiménez (1881), Martínez Sierra (1881).

Gonzalo Torrente Ballester adopts a flexible attitude toward the problem of fitting Benavente into one group or another. He considers him part of the Generation of '98 for some reasons, and a Modernist for others: "When . . . *The Witches' Sabbath* opened, those in the Generation of '98 recognized themselves in Benavente's play and took it as theirs."[5]

Nevertheless, on another occasion, Torrente Ballester speaks of certain differences of social level, education and attitude between Benavente and the rest of the Generation, differences which continued to separate them: "In spite of the initial friendship, in spite of the fact that *The Witches' Sabbath* is the first theatrical success of the Generation of '98, Benavente soon draws away from his early friends, as he draws away from their artistic way of life." Continuing, he says something about *The Witches' Sabbath* which apparently contradicts what he had previously said: ". . . the aesthetic similarities are few, but profound: the work cited is a Modernist play." This does not prevent him from adding: "But not for this reason does he cease to belong to the Generation of '98, to follow, in his own way and with his peculiar style, similar paths. As in Unamuno, Baroja, Valle-

[50]

Inclán, as in almost all of them, we find in Benavente a definite eagerness for individuality and a polemic attitude toward contemporary society."[6]

On another occasion he reaffirms the idea: "Benavente does not agree with his fellow members of the Generation of '98 in his attitude toward the problem of Spain, nor does the basis of his ideology maintain any relationship with those of Machado, Unamuno, Valle-Inclán or Azorín. Yet, the conclusions are often the same."[7] Domingo Pérez Minik does not fully agree with Azorín's statement that Benavente is the playwright of the Generation of '98, although he adds: "We can agree with it so far as Benavente implies a renovation and even a profound and lasting change in technique and in the conception of theatrical reality."[8]

Angel Valbuena Prat recognizes that Benavente's work is related to both movements, although he is more inclined to include him among the Modernists. Benavente, he says, "did not protest at being called a '98'er' and I believe that he considered himself a member of that generation . . . There is undoubtedly a relationship between his first plays, and some later ones, and the essence of the group which Azorín defined. In some, like *Well-Known People* and *Food for Wild Beasts*, there appears an attitude of criticism and discontentment with turn-of-the-century society. The same attitude appears in some articles in "Table Talk."[9] Nevertheless, speaking of Benavente's plays with a rural Castilian setting, plays which might have allowed him to come closer to the attitude of the Generation of '98, he states that Benavente has withdrawn considerably ". . . from the world of Unamuno, Baroja, Azorín, Maeztu or Antonio Machado. No one would think of any of these names, reading the village drama of *La malquerida (The Ill-Beloved)* or the shocking incest of *La infanzona (The Noblewoman)* . . . or even the play about daily life with a happy ending *Señora ama (The Lady of the House)*, the one which might have been closest to the atmosphere preferred by the Generation of '98. From all this, we see, in spite of certain differences, more relationship to Modernism than the true spirit of the Generation of '98."[10]

Andrés González Blanco, discussing Benavente's poetry, says: ". . . that Modernist gallantry which was already running rampant in the streets never reached Benavente . . . All of his artistic technique, his *manière de faire,* is based exclusively on Campoamor and Bécquer . . . there is no aesthetic nor prosodic innovation to take note of in Benavente; he who was to be a great innovator in the theater, never was such in poetry."[11]

Guillermo Díaz Plaja adopts a clear attitude toward the problem. In his work *Modernismo frente a Noventa y Ocho (Modernism Compared with the Generation of '98),* he tries to establish a definite line of differentiation between the two movements and states that "Modernism is a reaction against the Generation of '98, a different answer to the basic questions of an earlier generation . . ."[12] He posits the year 1902 as the date of the appearance of Modernism in Spain; considers "antigenerationism," aestheticism, and amoralism typical of the Modernist attitude and, according to him, also typical of Benavente's work. He says that it has not been shown that Benavente's attitude agrees with the moral, patriotic and sociological attitudes of the Generation of '98, adding that "Benavente stands opposed to these attitudes," and comes to the conclusion that "Benavente was, in the historic crossroads we are studying, 1895-1905, simply and resolutely a Modernist."[13]

I *Benavente as Seen by His Contemporaries*

Reading Benavente's turn-of-the-century plays today, it is difficult for the present-day reader to realize what they might have meant in their time. The impression we receive from these plays is undoubtedly very different from the one they caused at their premières. Even knowing the reactions of Benavente's contemporaries, there arises again the initial problem: the difficulty implicit in a strict and definitive categorization of the writer.

Azorín unquestionably considers Benavente a part of the Generation of '98 because of his role as innovator and revolutionary: "It may be said that the distinguishing characteristic of that generation, its dominant quality, was a profound love of art, a deep desire to protest against previous formulas and a desire for independence. The theater which was just beginning— Benavente's—marked a total revolution in Spanish drama."[14] He even says that "in the Generation of '98 . . . the figure of Benavente is perhaps the foremost."[15]

[52]

Antonio Machado, writing of the première of *Well-Known People,* after very favorable comments about the play, says:

All that means that Benavente was undertaking the greatest revolution in drama that our literature has ever known. So much greater, in fact, because it was a revolution which did not sound like one. A revolution with no shouting, convulsions, explosions, and uproars; more than this, it was a revolution against shouting, convulsions, and uproar, against all that false, pseudo-Romantic tinsel that was then plaguing the Spanish stage. It was a revolution of the discreet and the logical against the foolishness raised as a commonplace in the theater; of the real and the human against the fantastic and the silly; of quietness and depth against hollowness and shrillness; of the truth against conventional phantasmagoria . . . The public in 1896 wasn't ready to receive the novelty without wondering a little, but only a little, about the sudden change which had come about behind the curtains. Unfortunately, the critics were even less ready, and didn't help at all. Soon, however, the public, and the critics shortly thereafter, embraced the new theater, if not with exquisite taste, at least with unconditional enthusiasm.[16]

Unamuno, whose spirit was so different from Benavente's, also felt great admiration for his plays:

I am one of those who believe that there is no one today who can surpass our Benavente as a playwright, that his work is at least as good as that of Sudermann or Hauptmann, and yet, Benavente does not enjoy in Europe the critical reputation of Hauptmann and Sudermann nor has he been as widely translated as they. This is primarily due to the fact that Spain cannot put behind Benavente's *The Bonds of Interest* the cannons and armored ships which Germany put behind Hauptmann's *La campana sumergida (The Submerged Bell).*[17]

Benavente was one of the best-known and the most regular member of the *tertulias* of writers who met in the cafés of Madrid in the last years of the past century, around 1898. There they heatedly discussed everything: literature, art, politics, and religion. These *tertulias* have been considered an important factor in the appearance and growth of the Generation of '98.

Ricardo Baroja, in an article which appeared in 1923, gives us details of these meetings. He states that the uniform character which the group had at the beginning was gradually being lost:

[53]

"In the Café de Madrid two tendencies were becoming evident, and, consequently, two groups which tended to draw apart from each other. One, led by Benavente, who carried with him those who admired him for his stage writings; the other group, led by Valle-Inclán, revolutionary, undisciplined, rebellious . . . In Benavente's group almost all were literateurs; in Valle-Inclán's motley group, we may imagine writers, caricaturists, comedians, painters, and a student or two."[18] Ramón Gómez de la Serna, in his biography of Azorín, also speaks of these groups in similar terms.

II   The Cultural Background of Spanish Literature at the Beginning of the Century

From these quotes and from many other comments by Benavente's contemporaries, it may be deduced that at the beginning of the century Spanish writers and artists felt united by common, although ill-defined, restlessness and worries, motivated by a deep dissatisfaction and unhappiness with much which surrounded them. In the beginning, any new attitude toward Spain, past or present, attracted and stimulated them, whether it was the historical and cultural preoccupations of Ganivet and Unamuno or Darío's new forms of artistic expression. All of this was the result of the rebellious restlessness of young men who loved Spain very much, of a new generation which reacted with a strong critical spirit against the past, against all that was old. The new stylistic orientation of the Modernists, and the not quite so new critical revisions of things Spanish made by some writers concerned with defining the essence of Spain, and at the same time reaffirming their own identity, fit perfectly into the direction of reform.

These two attitudes which in the beginning had shared common concerns soon began to differentiate themselves. Each writer, following the dictates of his own temperament and inclination, took his own road, at times fusing the two orientations in his works, particularly in the beginning, as in the case of Valle-Inclán, Antonio Machado and Benavente.

At the turn of the century, these young and restless writers did not have a clear idea of what they were looking for. As Azorín wrote, "the Generation of '98 was not a political movement, but an attempt at a change in sensibility, which is impossible to change suddenly. Nevertheless, it is feasible to make an attempt at it. Those of the Generation of '98 didn't know what they were doing; they found it out later . . ."[19] They had no plan outlined, no program to follow. Like all authentic artists they sought only the most adequate means of expressing their feelings, of shaping the dark, subconscious impulses which always determine artistic creation. Only their discontent and their inability to adapt to their surroundings united them.

It has only been afterwards, with everything which has been said and written about these questions, that the different attitudes have become more sharply defined. But, by starting from two concepts, Modernism and the Generation of '98, which have been reshaped with time, have come to acquire meanings very different from those which they originally had. Even though their meaning today is still vague and ambiguous, it is nevertheless sufficiently clear that we may understand each other, up to a point, in using them.

III   *Benavente's Modernism*

In Benavente's case, it is interesting to remember the attitude which he himself adopted toward the term "Modernism" and those who, at the turn of the century, were called "Modernists." In *Fantasy Plays* (1892), one of the short dialogues is called "Modernism," with the sub-title of "New Forms." The characters are "A New Writer" and a "Modernist." Here is a selection:

MODERNIST. . . . If we keep on talking about Modernism we will never understand each other. I know of no one in Spain who has been officially declared a Modernist (nor anything like it). These words are invented by critics and reviewers, in their desire to put everyone into pigeonholes, and after they have invented them, they throw them in your face like an insult. Modernism, believe me, is just another word. A comfortable word, like all words, because it harbors so many ideas . . . the question of Modernism is very old. At any moment there is modernism, as there is old age or youth in the world; the fact that youth may be in opposition to the ideas of old age doesn't mean that the ideas of youth are new; it is enough that they are different . . . It is the eternal spirit of rebellion. But in art, laugh at labels and schools; all genres are good, the bad thing is those who insist on genres.

WRITER. Then, you think that Modernism, the new forms . . .

MODERNIST. Just a lot of talk! It's not a matter of breaking out of old patterns, only of widening them . . .[20]

Benavente uses the term "modernism" in a sense very different from that which has since been used in literature. But the fact is that in his time the word surely had the meaning he gives to it: that of something new, or modern. It apparently was applied to anything new, or what seemed to be new, whether it was a new literary style or the newest fanciful way of dressing. In *Vilanos (The Down of the Thistle)*, 1905, in the dialogue "A Choice of Clothing," the characters say:

COUNTESS. The traditional style of dress is too much for me. I prefer some modernist caprice.
COUNT. For Heaven's sake! . . . Don't look like an advertisement for cigarette paper or some item like that. Get away from modernism and its dangers.[21]

Benavente also makes ironic references to Modernism in *Teatro feminista (Plays About Women)*, 1898, a musical play in one act,[22] in *Food for Wild Beasts* (1898),[23] and in *Al natural (As It Is)*, 1903.[24] The dates of the premières of these plays are very significant.

Nevertheless, there is no doubt that Benavente, from the beginning of his literary career, had a definite inclination toward the movement which today is called "Modernism." Much of what he wrote has the unmistakable stamp which the works of Rubén Darío left on Spanish letters at the beginning of this century. In *Fantasy Plays,* there is a frivolity, a lightness, a concern with form and an aesthetic sensibility which is reminiscent of the spirit and form of Darío's prose and poetry. In *Figulinas* (1898), short tales and dialogues, there are also prose selections which echo the artifice of Modernism. In one of the dialogues, "Royal Wedding," Benavente describes the Princess:

The Princess is eighteen. Tall, slender, with a languid abandon in her body, an expression of weary and unutterable melancholy, like a tree, its branches moving in the wind, which feels the futile trembling of its roots, buried deep within the earth. White, of a soft, luminous whiteness; her blue eyes like petals of forget-me-nots; her smooth, blond hair caressed by a single ray of sunlight, burnished by a single brush stroke of gold. Her dress is simple, of pale pink, with no adornment other than a single ribbon of reddish-brown velvet, fastened with a cameo surrounded by turquoises.[25]

In a similar tone, he describes another character from "The Mad Virgins":

Pepita Castorjeriz, nineteen. Nervous, delicate as a small English hound. The incessant movement of her whole body contrasts with the inexplicable coldness of her face; like a sad clown, with a rigid face beneath the heavy mass of white lead . . . Seated at the piano, she muses over a French song of the eighteenth century, an expressive *marivaudage* of exaggerated love, like a bustle of Madame Pompadour. The harmony sought by Pepita with artificial evocation, calms her mind and her nerves, more excited than ever. The yellow of dusk penetrates the foilage of some tall, leafy Indian chestnuts, through the windows of her sitting room which open onto a damp, dark garden walled in by the houses bordering on the Castrojeriz' palace. The dark folds of the curtains shut out the last rays of the dying sun, as it is reflected on the brilliant silk of delicate colors. The old song sighs of loves of other times and Pepita, in that slow, harmonious twilight which surrounds her, prolongs the twilight of her soul, in which something intimate and profound is fading away forever. She wants to suspend her thoughts, to put them to sleep, to sweeten the inevitable farewell.[26]

In "Circus Poem," from *The Down of the Thistle,* Benavente comes dangerously close to saccharine sentimentality, which is repeated in many of his works and which, today, seems to us rather "corny":

MUSIC. From on high there come falling, expressionless in rhythm, without warmth in their artistic soul, as from an impersonal instrument, weeping waltzes played by a mechanical orchestra which rock the soul from the eyes to the heart, the heart to the eyes. Music which evokes memories of life long past . . . The memory of loves courted by it, of dances, affairs of other years and other places. The waltz learned in the intimacy of love, the waltz heard in a Parisian café concert, the only spiritual memory of one of those loves which leave only a golden memory, a head of golden hair, golden wines, gold coins . . . Music which evokes memories of the past, which rocks the soul between the heart and the eyes . . .[27]

The Modernist echo of Darío resounds even more clearly in "A vision of Old," from the same work, *The Down of the Thistle:*

The height of human beauty, glory and power: Elagabal, child of the sun, and like the sun, resplendent over all the earth; he wears a heavenly garment, with stars of gold and jewels embroidered on tunic and mantle; from the imperial palace, among beautiful things, young colossi, caressed and defended, wrapped in a blue mist of perfumes, he smiles between sips of frozen Cypress at the green and blue, red and gold guides of the quadriga, as among clouds of dust tinted with gold and red, they renew the races of the Homeric heroes in the funeral games of Patroclus.[28]

In these selections, and in many others which could be quoted, the influence on Benavente of the new Modernist sensibility which had come to Spain with Darío's first works can clearly be seen. It was an influence reinforced by the visit of the Nicaraguan poet to Spain, where he had arrived in 1898, making friends with the best writers of that period, including those of the Generation of '98.

Of course, Modernism is an essentially poetic phenomenon, whether in prose or verse, and doesn't fit well into dramatic dialogue. For this reason it appears more clearly in Benavente in the prose which he wrote to be read rather than in his theatrical dialogues. The form and spirit of Modernism, cold, lacking in humanity and clearly artificial, alienate it from the essence of drama and human conflict. Nevertheless, we find echoes of Modernism in the theater of Benavente; and of Valle-Inclán, in *La cabeza del dragon (The Dragon's Head)*, or in *Voces de gesta (Epic Voices)*; also in the theater of Francisco Villaespesa (1877-1946), superficially exotic, decadent and affected in *El alcázar de las perlas (The Castle of Pearls)*, 1911. (Villaespesa is authentically Modernist in his poetry, in *La copa del rey Thule (King Thule's Cup)* [1900].) There is also a trace of Modernism, with traditional motifs, in the work of Eduardo Marquina (1879-1946), *El monje blanco (The White Monk)*, while Luis Fernández Ardavín (b.1892) cultivated a belated Modernism in *La dama de armiño (The Lady in Ermine)*, 1921. One may even speak of Modernist elements in the early works of so independent a writer as Jacinto Grau.

Benavente not only shows some relation to Modernism in the selections from his work just cited, but he also participated actively in the propagation of the new style, helping and encouraging the young writers who tried the new formulas. He was editor and director of the review *Vida literaria (Literary Life)*, which appeared in January of 1899, with clearly revolutionary tendencies, open to all the winds of change. According to words, surely its director's, which appeared in the journal, "*Literary Life* is open to any manifestation of art, with no preferences for labels or schools; old or young, reactionary or liberal, idealist or positivist." Rubén Darío, Gregorio Martínez Sierra, Manuel Machado, Leopoldo Alas (Clarín), Armando Palacio Valdés, Eduardo Zamacois, Miguel de Unamuno, Ramiro de Maeztu and other less well-known writers collaborated in its production.

This is to say that Benavente may be considered not only as one who cultivated the new Modernist styles, but also as one who turned the young writers of that period toward the new tendencies. Rubén Darío himself considered Benavente to be within his artistic movement, yet at the same time recognized his clearly Spanish accent, in saying: "This Modernist is as pure and noble in his writing and speaking as the antiquity of certain jewels or lace, as Velásquez sleeves or Pantoja jewels."[29]

IV   *The Separation of Modernism and the Generation of '98*

The Modernist influence on Spanish literature at the beginning of the century was of considerable importance. The revolutionary tendency of the writers of the Generation of '98 brought with it a demand for a reform of language and style. The Modernist movement was traveling the same road, and although they later drew away from what this movement represented, in the beginning it reached almost all of them to a greater or lesser degree, even, (marginally) to writers like Unamuno whose often careless style seems opposed to Modernist exquisiteness and artificiality.

Pedro Salinas even comes to the conclusion that the language of Modernism was "the official language of the new generation." Although later, he says, the writers of the Generation of '98 "discovered the basic contradiction which existed between what

Modernism implied of a materialistic, sensual and unconventional view of life, and the austere and serious spiritual questioning of those of the Generation of '98 . . . Once the old idols had been knocked over, the temporary allies, Modernism and the Generation of '98, broke apart, in natural obedience to their very different *raisons d'être*. With this rupture they demonstrated the essence of their differences."[30]

There was not only a division or separation between the Modernists and those of the Generation of '98. In spite of the revolutionary restlessness which united the men of '98 in the beginning, each one followed his own road. Because all of them were writers of great individuality, each one produced his own very personal and unique work. They did not make up what is commonly referred to as a "literary school," as had happened with the Modernists. To the extreme that from an artistic or literary point of view, and even more from a human point of view, characteristics which differentiated the writers commonly included in the Generation of '98 from each other are much clearer and more meaningful than those which united them. Because of the magical—or mythical—power which accepted literary labels have, almost all studies published on the Generation of '98 emphasize the analogies and similarities, ignoring the differentiating and often more significant aspects.

In closing, then, we can conclude from all we have just said that the same fundamental preoccupations existed in Benavente which stimulated other writers of his time; a desire to reform, to change, a reaction against the old and outdated. In these attempts at reform, in his discontent with the theater of his time, in his artistic restlessness, Benavente lies within the reforming, revolutionary attitude of the Generation of '98.

On the other hand, Benavente, because of his temperament, his essential *madrileñismo* (he was the only true *madrileño* by birth and sentiment in the group), and because of the social level at which he lived as a satisfied, socially conservative and elegantly dressed bourgeois, was very different from his fellow members of the Generation of '98. In Baroja, Valle-Inclán, Azorín, Machado, and Unamuno, there was a certain rather Bohemian unconventionality, an inability to adapt themselves to the society in which they lived. Benavente was moving away from his fellows for these reasons and because his artistic career as a popular playwright who wished to go on pleasing his well-off audience alienated him from the more serious preoccupations of the other writers of the Generation of '98.

Also, to a greater extent, there were in Benavente clear temperamental and stylistic similarities with the practices of Darío, particularly at the beginning of his literary career: scrupulous concern for form, artificiality, coldness, a certain artistic decadence and moral indifference, and a lack of concern for political or social problems.

Because of all this, following the now firmly established custom of pigeonholing writers into neat little groups with classifying labels, one must come to the conclusion that Benavente fits better among the Modernists than among the writers of the Generation of '98. Yet, one should never lose sight of the arbitrary, artificial and fallacious character of such classifications.

CHAPTER 4

A Classification of His Works

IT is very difficult to classify Benavente's plays, especially if one wants to make a classification into clearly differentiated groups.

There are two obstacles which stand in the way of carrying out such a classification. First, the number of plays he wrote, one hundred and seventy-two. Secondly, their great variety, the lack of homogeneity which is found even in plays which, from one point of view, might be grouped together. In some of them one may, with little effort, find important characteristics by which they could be included in another group.

The diversity of Benavente's dramatic production is confusing. Guillermo Díaz-Plaja justifiably claims that "Reading and seeing his plays presented, we have often thought of mercury: fluid, inapprehensible, slippery, brilliant, cold. It is, to begin with, impossible to reduce Benavente's theater to a formula."[1]

All of the published studies on Benavente when they attempt to classify his plays, clearly show uncertainty and confusion. Even in 1916 Andrés González Blanco was saying: "In the beginning of his career it was possible to classify Benavente as a writer of comedies; today he is impossible to classify. The satiric vein was what he first handled so well; later he turned to light, drawing room comedy; he has at last turned to drama, but has not failed to try his hand at theater of all sorts: *zarzuelas* (musical comedies), comic farces, monologues, proverbs."[2]

For this reason the classifications made by the critics cover rather ill-defined groups which in no case include all of the author's works. There always remain a great number of them which can be indiscriminately placed in one or another group, or which do not fit into any group.

Domingo Pérez Minik tries to divide his plays into three broad groups: "All of Benevente's theater, of so many forms, since it includes everything from the fable to the dramatized novel, including the *sainete,* the *zarzuela* and the cinedrama, can be reduced to (1) the purely psychological play, like *The Intruder;* (2) the satire on manners or politics with a moral intent, like *The Bonds of Interest;* and lastly (3) the ideological drama with a spectacular purpose, like *The Witches' Sabbath.*"[3]

This classification fails to include some of Benevente's best plays, like *The Ill-Beloved* or *The Lady of the House;* his plays for children; fantasy plays; his translations and adaptations; the "sentimental" and purely comic plays. Indeed, the concept of "the ideological drama with a spectacular purpose" is too vague, and very few of his plays could fall into this category. *The Witches' Sabbath,* indeed, is unique among Benevente's plays.

Federico Sáinz de Robles attempts a more detailed classification: "In my opinion, Benevente's theater comprises three perfectly determined groups: a) realistic plays, b) fantasy plays, and c) translations and adaptations. The realistic plays may be subdivided into comedies of manners, social satires, character plays and dramas; the fantasy plays, into children's plays or fairy tale plays, and symbolic plays."[4]

Continuing, Sáinz de Robles points out the plays which, according to him, are the outstanding ones in each group. His is an incomplete classification, about as arbitrary as any other. Citing the outstanding plays in each group, he broadens the category of symbolic plays with another very questionable category. He calls them "symbolic plays or plays with psychological themes," and he includes in this group such diverse works as *The Witches' Sabbath* and *The Bonds of Interest.*

Angel Valbuena Prat believes that Benevente's theater may be divided among "rural dramas, like *The Ill-Beloved, The Lady of the House* and *The Noblewoman;* a poetical-satirical theater, the outstanding example of which is *The Bonds of Interest;* and 'high comedy' or 'drawing room comedy.' This category would be the broadest and most easily subdivided."[5]

Without exception, the classifications which have been made until now of Benevente's plays only point out a few in each group. Even so, a play included in one group often could easily be included in another. In Benavente's theater such a lack of precision is irremediable.

The classification which I am making tries to include all of Benavente's works. I realize the risk involved in such an undertaking and the relative and provisional merit of the result. Such a classification must necessarily be flexible. If anyone does not agree with the inclusion of some play in a particular category, he may include it in another. The classification must be considered, then, as an attempt at a general orientation, as a tentative guide.

This classification also includes a personal evaluation of the plays. I place the works I consider to be the best at the beginning of each group; and at the last, the less worthy. These reach a considerable proportion, as is to be expected in so prolific a writer.

Classification

(For a chronological listing of the plays the reader is referred to the Appendix.)

Satirical plays:
  The Bonds of Interest, Well-Known People, Little Man, The Thing to Do, The Evildoers of Good, Food for Wild Beasts, The Governor's Wife, Pin Pricks, The Angora Cat, Another Kind of Honor, Mrs. Téllez' Husband, Toward the Truth, And It Was Bitter . . . , Abdication, For Heaven and Altar, The Sons Are as Fathers, The New Sons-in-law, Web of Lies, The Devil of the Theater, Virtue Is Suspect, Cousin Roman, A Husband in Bronze, When the Children of Eve Are not the Children of Adam, These Things Are Not to Be Played With, Literature, The Happy and Confident City.

Psychological Plays:
  The Intruder, Pepa Doncel, The Evil They Do Us, The School for Princesses, Snow in May, In Love with Love, Needles in the Mouth, Lessons on Love, Behind Closed Doors, The Devil Was Once an Angel, Nor Love Nor Sea, Bread Eaten from the

Hand, His Wife's Rival, Truth Invented, Sacrifices, The Sorrow-ful City, Titania, Divorce of the Soul, Don Juan Has Arrived, Why Is Love?, After All, a Woman, From a Very Good Family, You, Once and The Devil, Ten.

Rural Plays:

The Ill-Beloved The Lady of the House, The Noblewoman.

Fantasy Plays:

Fantasy Plays (eight short plays meant to be read rather than staged), *The Snow-Bride, A Night of Lights, The Gypsy Duch-ess, To Serve, Fire Dragon.*

Comedies (Light, comic plays; a few with satirical tone):

His Widow's Husband, The Moral of Divorce, It's Your Fault, No One Knows What He Wants, or The Dancer and the Laborer, Don Magín the Magician, Little Red Riding Hood Frightens the Wolf, Anyone Knows That, As It Really Is, The Cicada-Ants, The Automobile, The Train for Married Men.

Sentimental Plays (Plays of a sentimentality which often borders on "corniness"):

Self-Esteem, Stronger than Love, Field of Ermine, The Neck-lace of Stars, The Grave of Dreams, The Cubs.

Miscellaneous Plays (There is no distinguishing characteristic. Some of them could be included in one of the groups already mentioned. Others could perhaps form a new group):

The Witches' Sabbath, Autumnal Roses, Honor Among Men, Hamlet's Fool, Mater Imperatrix, The Vestal Virgin of the West, The Immaculate of Sorrows, A Woman of the Poor, The Un-believable, Crossed Lives, Brute Force, Loyal to All, A Traitor to All, Imprisoned Souls, Rags of the Royal Purple, Manon Lescault, The Hound of Heaven, The Butterfly Who Flew Over the Sea, I Don't Want To, Memoirs of a Citizen of Madrid, A Lady, The Children's Law, The Soul Triumphant, Polichinela's Son, The Eyes of the Dead, Life in Verse, To Save His Love, Adoration, Among the Clouds, The Lady in Mourning, The Last Letter, Beyond Death, Holy Russia, The Owls, A Jazz-Band Melody, Birds of a Feather.

Minor Works (almost all short, one-act plays. Dialogues, monologues, tableaux, *sainetes* with or without music, brief comic farces, *zarzuelas* and plays for children. Many of them, because of their content, could be placed in the groups already mentioned):

At the Gates of Heaven, Truth, Light Mourning, For Small Reasons, An Image of Greatness, Style, The Understudy, Don Juan's Servant, The House of Good Fortune, Who's Afraid of Love?, Up Close, A Female Mephistopheles, We Are All One, At the Service of Her Imperial Majesty, The Princess Without a Heart, Love Must Be Sent to School, No Smoking, Man's Friends, Plays about Women, A Surgical Operation, Cruel Goodby, An Apprentice's Journey, Through the Wound, Unintentionally, The Favorites, The Countess' Fright, An Immoral Story, Grandmother and Granddaughter, The Enchanted Cup, The Smile of Mona Lisa, The Story of Othello, The Last Minuet, The Young Lady Is Bored, What Can a Man Do!, The Grandson, Why John Quit Drinking, A Pair of Boots, The Suicide of Lucerito, Do You Think I Like It?, His Loving Wife, Grandfather and Grandson, Darling Daughter!, Children Lost in the Forest.

Children's Theater:

And Now a Story . . . , Cinderella, The Prince Who Learned Everything from Books, To Earn a Living.

Translations and Adaptations:

King Lear, from Shakespeare's play; *A Tale of Love,* from Shakespeare's *Twelfth Night, or What You Will; Don Juan,* from Molière's play *Le Festin de Pierre; Mademoiselle Belle-isle,* from a play by A. Dumas, père; *Richelieu,* from the play by Bulwer-Lytton; *A Good Marriage,* from the play *Un Beau Mariage* by E. Augier; *Destiny Calls,* from a play by Paul Hervieu, *The Yellow Tunic,* from the play by G. G. Hazelton and H. Benrimo; *Freedom!,* a translation of the play in Catalan by Santiago Rusiñol; *The Bold One,* an adaptation of Galdós' novel.

In all there are twenty-seven satirical plays, twenty-three psychological plays, three rural plays, seven fantasy plays, eleven comic plays, six sentimental plays, thirty-five miscellaneous works, forty-nine short plays and eleven translations and adaptations: a total of 172 plays. They were written during sixty active years as a playwright (1894-1954). To all this should be added his non-dramatic works, *Letters from Women* (1893); *Figurines* (1898); *The Down of the Thistle* (1905); a book of poetry, *Poems* (1893). We add also his extensive journalistic and critical works which fill several volumes.

Benavente's excessive fertility hurt him. He wrote a great many plays without dedicating sufficient time to them. But because of his great prestige they were well received by the impresarios and the public, and Benavente always felt flattered to see his name continuously on the theater marquees. There was, besides, a purely economic reason, to which he makes reference in one of his articles: "In order to receive even a small income from his plays an author must keep on producing without respite. He runs the risk of falling into repetition and carelessness."[6] The problem is very serious in Spain where even a good play often has only a short stage run. This has always hurt Spanish theater in general and the best authors in particular, who find themselves forced to write too much in order to live by their pen.

CHAPTER 5

Themes

THE thematic content of Benavente's dramas is implicit in their classification. In order to be more precise, it may be useful to point out the predominant themes in each of the two most characteristic groups, the satirical and the psychological, and the way in which Benavente uses these themes.

I *Satirical Plays*

The plays of satiric intent are the most numerous and are those which, more than any other group, are most characteristic of Benavente's art. His is a satire that touches most aspects of Spanish social life, and even on occasion goes beyond the national context; high society in Madrid: *Well-Known People, Food for Wild Beasts, Little Man, The Angora Cat, Abdication, The New Sons-in-law, Virtue is Suspect.* There are themes involving provincial life and politics: *The Evildoers of Good, Pin Pricks, Web of Lies, A Husband in Bronze, The Governor's Wife, Cousin Roman.* The theme of the bankrupt aristocracy appears in *The Sons Are as Fathers, The New Sons-in-law.* There are plays on life in the theater *(Mrs. Téllez' Husband, And It Was Bitter . . . , The Devil and the Theater),* on man's search for happiness *(Princess Bebé),* on the morality of modern society *(When the Children of Eve Are Not the Children of Adam, These Things Are Not to Be Played With, Another Kind of Honor).* We find the delicate religious theme *(For Heaven and Altar),* the theme of literary life *(Literature),* and the moral-philosophical satire *(The Bonds of Interest).*

Benavente's satire is essentially social. It is life in society that is the theme upon which his satirical irony is focussed. Nevertheless, it is not a theater of "social problems." Benavente was not a revolutionary writer. On the contrary, he was a conservative, self-satisfied bourgeois, a *señorito* who found himself very much at home in the society he criticized.

He chose to concentrate on the minor problems of his society. Ignoring the really important ones, it was as though they had never existed. He did not see them; he refused to see them. Undoubtedly attempting to justify himself, he even comes to make such absurd statements as " . . . Spanish life is so calm and peaceful that it scarcely provides the dramatist a source for his material. There is no need to think about social problems, for they interest no one. We already know that no problems exist in Spain. The religious question is only a pretext for political programs . . . Social problems, in the end, turn out to be, as a famous actor said of a certain play in which he had acted, 'Hunger and gunshots, things which are always unpleasant.'"[1]

The key to Benavente's attitude in relation to authentic social problems is to be found in this last statement: he avoids presenting deeply unpleasant, or what he considered deeply unpleasant, things on stage, those things which were also unpleasant for the comfortable audience who applauded his plays. For him, unpleasantness is the misery, hunger and suffering of the poor; the violence provoked by social injustice, the class struggle. He also avoided portraying great passion or the violence of dramatic conflict which might be associated with this unpleasantness.

Hence Benavente's theater is essentially bourgeois and self-satisfied at heart in spite of his apparent nonconformity. His is not a "committed" theater, a theater of *engagement*. This is explained, in part, by the fact that he always lived in economic well-being. His youth was that of a typical *señorito* of Madrid, well-educated, well-dressed, elegant. During the rest of his life he lived always among wealthy people, in the highest levels of the Madrid society which treated him with great affection. He felt ill at ease among people of lower social levels. He had little contact with the masses, the working class.

For this reason he never intended to change the society he criticized, a refined but decadent bourgeois society, content with itself and interested, above all, in maintaining its own privileges in the status quo. Benavente is interested only in the past and the present; he never worries about the future. He is conservative by temperament, conservative in his principles, and conservative because it was to his own advantage. His work and his personality are at the opposite extreme from Galdós, who is an authentic revolutionary. As a result, Benavente's satire is amiable in essence, although it occasionally seems harsh. It is a theater of bourgeois conformity.

The social group at which his theater was directed, the same group that he criticized and who attended the performance of his plays, accepted his satire because he never reached the point of upsetting the spectator's digestion with his bittersweet barbs. It is true, however, that his satire occasionally becomes harsh and that he does not condone certain attitudes, situations or character types. He exposes the moral decadence, hypocrisy and snobbery of high society in bold and frank words. Yet in the course of his exposé he always wears an indulgent and amiable smile behind his mask of disapproval. Benavente seems to shrug his shoulders at what he considers inevitable: the insincerity of man as a social being. The spectacle of appearances and reality in which the characters of his plays become involved seems, rather, to amuse him. There is no indignation in his voice. He is no dry and stern moralist. He is only a witness, an observer, a *costumbrista*, yet his *costumbrismo* is nearly always urbane and tactful. He softens his attack with a generous dose of frivolity and humor. The audience smiles in sympathy with him.

The technique of his presentation is perfectly suited to the sophisticated atmosphere of the elegant salons he criticizes: a carefully constructed, "literary," clever dialogue where much is said but very little happens, where good manners are seldom abandoned. The audience was entertained by his antics and was never hurt by them. They were taken as a joke by a mischievous and clever writer, never in bad taste. His tact is admirable. He takes great care to assure that most of what happens occurs offstage, never in full view. As Princess Bebé says in the play of her name: "The important things occur behind the scenes." It is precisely these manipulations behind the social screen, behind the curtain of social conventions which are expressed in his satirical plays in the form of conversation.

The society which he satirizes was clearly decadent. Benavente knew this intuitively. It was a society in a state of crisis, a society in the process of change, where hypocrisy reigned and which Benavente only half unmasked. Occasionally there appears a gesture of rebellion against tradition, for example, the attitude of Nené in *El hombrecito (Little Man)*. Benavente foresaw the need for a series of changes which were indeed, in part, later effected. Benavente, however, only suggests or implies them, without attacking their causes or examining their consequences.

At times, on rare occasions, his attack takes on a serious note and becomes more profound, as in *Los malhechores del bien (The Evildoers of Good)*, December 1, 1905, where he touches on one aspect of the "social problem." It is a strong attack on false charity in an atmosphere dominated by hypocrisy and vested social and religious interests. The action takes place in a small town. The poor people are manipulated by some ladies of the upper class who consider themselves very Christian and charitable, but who demand unconditional submission from the poor whom they help. They only attend to a few whom they consider "good" according to their narrow and false points of view, and they look down on those who do not follow the norms which they have imposed. There appears in the play a very interesting character, Heliodoro, the only one who speaks the truth.

The plot is very simple; it is centered around two poor young people of the region, Jesús and Natividad. They are sweethearts and are in love. But the "charitable" ladies oppose the marriage of Natividad to Jesús because he is a rebel who pays no attention to them and has even called them witches. They attempt to arrange the marriage of Natividad to Martín, a young man who obeys their fancy and their interests. But Don Heliodoro, together with his niece Teresa, arranges for Jesús and Natividad to run away, thus frustrating the ladies' plans.

The play was interpreted as a politically motivated denunciation, even as an attack on the clergy; its performance provoked reactions of displeasure among the audiences who saw it. Some ladies, in a gesture of protest, even left the theater. The subject produced a certain uneasiness in the audience because it bared to them certain truths which they didn't want to see. Benavente had gone beyond the line of what his audience considered "good taste." For this reason, perhaps a little frightened, he never repeated himself. He soon afterwards presented a lyric *sainete, The Understudy* (December 23, 1905); a comic farce, *The Cicada-Ants* (December 24, 1905), and a sentimental play set in an aristocratic atmosphere, *Stronger than Love* (February 22, 1906) in which the kindness and compassion of a woman are triumphant. The bad mood caused by *The Evildoers of Good* was soon forgotten.

Only twenty-three years later did he write another controversial play, *For Heaven and Altar* (1928), whose action is set among friars, ministers and kings. It is for Benavente quite a daring play, with clearly anti-clerical tone. There is a friar, with a reputation as a saint, who performs miracles in curing a prince who was believed to be dying. The people are restless and there are disturbances. The government expels the friars, and a minister at one point says, quoting the Papal Nuncio, "Saints are good only in heaven and on altars." In an epilogue, a republic has been declared in the imaginary country in which the action takes place. The saint has been canonized. A fiesta is celebrated in his honor, with a fair and entertainment. Now the saint is "in heaven and on the altars" and is not causing any problems.

The play's performance in the Teatro Eslava of Madrid was announced for the thirtieth of November, 1928. But it had already aroused dangerous comments. It was said that it was revolutionary and critical of the current political régime of Spain, the monarchy of Alfonso XIII, governed by General Primo de Rivera. The government banned it, although in an officially published note it gave permission for it to be printed. Naturally, it was widely sold and commented upon.

Yet the theme which Benavente employed and his manner of doing so went far afield of the type of play to which his audience was accustomed. He always wanted to avoid serious arguments and controversies over his plays. Evidently it did not seem to him to be useful seriously to disturb his audience with attacks which were too harsh. "His audience" was not only such because it attended the performance of his plays to spend a pleasant evening. It was his because Benavente himself formed a part of the same social group. He wrote from the same social level he criticized, directing his attacks, softened by humor and sentimentality, at his own friends and acquaintances.

A tabulation of his plays according to the characters used, that is, according to the social atmosphere they reflect, gives us the following result: plays with an aristocratic setting (kings, princes and nobles), twenty-six; plays with a setting among the upper class (wealthy people who associate with aristocrats), fifteen; upper middle class, forty-six; middle class, twenty-five; lower middle class, thirteen; provincial setting (he invented the city of Moraleda), eight. As can be seen, the plays with an upper class setting, almost two-thirds of his total production, clearly predominate. There is no doubt that Benavente was writing for his "special public." He wanted to keep it happy, without upsetting it with serious problems which might make it think too much. Of course, he tried not to irritate it. His is, then, to a certain extent, a theater of escape.

Yet Benavente himself was bothered by the displeased critics who commented unfavorably on his preference for aristocratic settings. "The majority of my critics," he says, "have always attempted to pigeonhole me. I was, they said, no more than a writer of comedies in an aristocratic setting, something to go with conversation and a cup of tea . . . Among my hundred or so plays, only about eight or ten have an aristocratic setting, and these are the ones which I have written with greatest dislike and the one which least satisfy me."[2]

Clearly, as our own tabulation above shows, his calculation stops far short of the actual number of plays with an aristocratic atmosphere. But if, as he says, he wrote them with great dislike, there is no other conclusion but that he tried to write them to the public's taste. This is made even clearer when Benavente goes on to speak of his plays with a middle-class setting: "My favorite (plays) are those with a popular, middle-class atmosphere, for this is the atmosphere I have known best . . . Now our stupid middle class, whose distinguishing characteristic has always been diffidence, *doesn't want to see itself portrayed seriously;* rather, it wants to see itself idealized, or it prefers to see itself ridiculed, which is also a means of idealization. Nonsense! If I wrote plays with an aristocratic setting it was, immodestly, as a lesson in writing them."³ (My italics). There are too many such plays to be considered only a lesson.

Again, in an article, he speaks on the same subject:

. . . in my plays I have, perhaps, managed to capture some aspects of life in Madrid, particularly of its middle class, which I have known best and *in which I live* . . . Madrid has a lot of character, with great virtues and great defects, and it must thus be judged. This is the way I have tried to picture it in my Madrid plays, which form the greatest part of all I have written. Madrid, like a great gentleman, has, among others, the virtue of remaining undisturbed by criticism. *I, would never have dared to say about a particular province the things I have dared to say about Madrid.* To speak of the provinces, I have my Moreleda, which is no one province in particular but is all of them together, at times even Madrid, which, in being Madrid, never ceases to be a province of Spain.⁴ (My italics)

From the content of his plays, and from his own words, it is clear that Benavente was always very careful not to say things clearly enough that they would provoke uncomfortable controversy. As a result, his satire, as we have remarked above, is smooth, amiable and indulgent. In this sense, he is an exception in Spanish literature. His satirical attacks are of a spirit very different from that of Quevedo, Larra, Cadalso, Ganivet, Baroja, and others. Satire in Spanish literature usually tends to be harsh and bitter. Benavente's satire is aseptic, calm, ironic, and only skin deep; it is a satire of a skepticism, tinted sometimes with melancholy, so innocuous that it destroys its own message in the end.

Benavente is a skeptic in the broadest sense of the word. He is as one might say, beyond good and evil. He believes in nothing, except perhaps in the inevitability of the defects of the social life he criticizes: hypocrisy, human falsity, selfishness. He does not believe, as did Ibsen for example, that the evils which corrupt society may be corrected. He is a skeptical and indifferent pessimist who offers no possible solution. There is in his work a certain moral indifference. Because of this some critics have attacked his work, considering it immoral and un-Christian. "Benavente," says José Vila Selma, "has the virtue of anchoring his work and its themes in the very flesh, infa-

mously awry, of the pagan body of our time. Herein lies his contemporaneity."[5]

This is, indeed, his contemporaneity—and much of the reason
for his success. His is not a case of amorality. His satires arise
from the comparison of two views of morality. On one side,
religious morality, outwardly accepted, according to him, in
society; on the other side, the morality of life, of instinct,
of feeling. The latter is usually triumphant in his plays, as in
life, but it is almost always hidden behind human hypocrisy.
And, as he doesn't believe in solutions nor in the efficacy of sermons, he limits himself to presenting his view of certain aspects
of human reality, in a social context, with irony and humor.
With this he often satirizes not only a particular social group,
but human hypocrisy and man himself.

The defects of the social setting he portrays are strongly em-
phasized. It is a polished, decadent society in need of reform,
a society molded and suffocated by moral and ethical norms
which no one takes seriously and which serve only as a kind of
smoke screen. For this reason many of his characters seem
amoral and cynical. The rebels in this society—Nené of *Little
Man* and the Princess Bebé, for example—seemed in Benavente's
day much more rebellious, alienated an even immoral. Today
they seem much less so.

In no case do these dissident characters acquire greatness;
the depth of emotion and passion which leads a protagonist to
death and destruction, has no place in his theater. Rebellious
characters are merely individuals with strong personalities who
serve only as a contrast to the atmosphere of which they form a
part. Nené ends up adapting herself to the environment against
which she had rebelled, and plays the game the others have imposed. One has only to recall her last words, which end the
play: "Nothing . . . , I have learned to live . . . , like everyone . . . and now you see . . . , I accept life . . ." That is, she
accepts life as Benavente saw it, as a game of deceit and falsity.

Because of all this, the thematic content of Benavente's theater is of a light tone. Except in two or three plays in which
there is intense drama touching on tragedy *(The Ill-Beloved,
The Noblewoman, The Witches' Sabbath)*, Benavente prefers to
avoid conflict, presenting to us only what may be called the

"small realities" of life in society, in what has been called
"drawing room" or "high" comedy. Here, in elegant salons,
among well-dressed and well-educated people, Benavente felt
at home. In this somewhat artificial and conventional setting,
they speak only of each other in an unending game of falsity
and deceit.

Dialogue, which, as has already been said, Benavente handles
with consummate skill, serves him as a means of presenting
character and atmosphere and to suggest small conflicts which
ultimately disappear. It is all stylized, worldly, clever, and
entertaining. It deals with critical observations of society, centered on the small individual problems of each character. His
thematic technique seeks above all, to capture atmosphere. For
this reason action disappears without getting to the bottom of
the problems, without bothering to analyze the causes. His
typical themes always border on the superficial and the pe-
ripheral, on what is reflected in the characters' words and attitudes. But at the same time, delicately and tactfully, he succeeds in circumscribing the themes he treats in such a way
that, together with an apparent dispersion, there is unity of
content, of intent, as I have said. Benavente achieves his goals
and succeeds in producing technically faultless plays in his own
style.

The thematic unity which Benavente successfuly injects into
his satirical and social plays is better appreciated if we consider
these two kinds of plays together. Each one of them really
treats one aspect of what is one large problem. In all of the
plays of this type he emphasizes with appropriate characters
and dialogue, a particular facet of his favorite theme: the falsity
and hypocrisy of man in society. In *The Bonds of Interest,* for
example, we have a philosophical-moral satire or a critical
philosophy of life, with no particular setting in time or space.
In *Well-Known People* we have a satire on the power of
money among people whose nobility lies solely in their name,
who hide behind their own misery and who bow to the new
aristocracy of money. *Little Man* affords a satire on the rebellion of a young woman against the hypocrisy which surrounds
her and who, at last vanquished by overwhelming pressure, follows the accepted game of pretense. *The Evildoers of God,*

as we saw above, is a satire on false goodness and charity. *Pin Pricks* has a somewhat similar theme: the protagonist, don Remigio, in spite of his good intentions, cannot use his money to "do good," because of the hypocrisy which surrounds him. *Food for Wild Beasts* presents a satire on the ingratitude of friends and servants, in the midst of known lies and hypocrisy, etc.

The unity of these satirical plays lies in their intent, and, thus considered, their lack of action is not a defect nor a limitation, since the important thing lies in the individual reaction, in the commentary of each character as a part of an amorphous whole. All is presented as a vast spectacle in which the characters' lack of morality, their hypocrisy and falseness, appear as intrinsic human characteristics arising out of an atmosphere created by the author with wit and truth.

Benavente confines himself to presenting such an atmosphere without making explicit moral judgements. He is only the critical observer who presents objectively what he sees around him, who offers his view, that aspect which interests him of human reality, shrugging his shoulders at the same time because he believes there is no solution. Tragedy cannot enter into such a view. The atmosphere of tragedy is alien to the author's skeptical smile. Seldom do there appear great feelings or storms of passion, and when they do arise they seem false and alien to his temperament and style. The passion and tragedy of *The Ill-Beloved* are an exception.

Likewise seem false the touches of optimism or tenderness which Benavente occasionally places at the end of some of his plays. The note of optimism or tenderness was undoubtedly a concession to the public, so that the barren social panorama he presents might not seem so desolate. For this reason the ending of *Little Man*—where hypocrisy and falseness are triumphant—or that of *Pin Pricks*—in which a disillusioned and defeated man is forced to abandon his good intentions—seems more consistent and convincing than that of *Another Kind of Honor* in which Victor's nobility and kindness succeed in weakening the will of his wife Julia, who repents and wants to begin her life anew; or the ending of some of the "sentimental" plays like *Stronger than Love* or *The Necklace of Stars*.

Benavente is well aware of all this:

If some label for my theater attracts me, it would be the theater of discretion . . . Violent, unrestrained passion is rarely found in theater. For this very reason they have accused me of coldness. Rarely has destiny, the fate of Greek tragdey, won out over free will in the souls of my characters. Prudence and reason always restrain passion and sentiment; the characters always stop to reflect, and reflection always wins out over the impulses of their passions.[6]

Because his is a theater of reason—particularly in the satirical and psychological plays—coldness, or detachment, is his greatest virtue and at the same time his greatest limitation. It is a virtue in that Benavente's satire does not admit sentiment or passion. It is a limitation in that it does not allow him to penetrate into the depths of the human soul and thus he must abjure the most profound and meaningful content. He is not concerned with man's inner and often desperate struggle with himself. He is at the opposite pole from the agony of Unamuno. He does not concern himself with the eternal questions of life, nor even with those pressing problems which arise out of hunger and social injustice. When the flesh of the fruit he bites into turns out to be a little bitter, he spits it out, or worse still, he puts a little honey or marmalade on it. In the plays in which sentiment plays a part, there is always too much sugar. When the sweetness is gone, the taste which is left is sour, acid, bittersweet, but never entirely bitter. Yet, taking all this into account one must recognize that he is a consummate master of his light superficial art.

II Psychological Plays

The plays included in this group also often have a satirical tone. But in the psychological plays, woman is the focal point; and the central theme around which the play revolves is that of love as seen by woman. It may be said that, in general terms, all of Benavente's theater has a feminine character. As a rule women occupy the center of his work. The only really strong characters he has created are feminine, as we will see in the next chapter on dramatic technique.

He portrays feminine love in all its facets: the love of mother, wife, sweetheart or mistress. At times, he expresses the resignation and sacrifice of the woman caught between emotion and duty; at other times, he examines the fickleness and inconstancy of her relationship with men, her strong desire to stand out in society, or her vigorous attempts to dominate. His feminine characters are always treated more sympathetically and are more clearly defined than the masculine characters.

In his very first play, *The Intruder,* the theme of love is delicately presented; it is really only intimated in characters who are not fully aware, until the end, of their real feelings. The play is a sober and simple one of very little action. There are only three central characters. A childless couple live with two servants. The husband, José Luis, a completely dedicated businessman, is a sickly hypochondriac who is always tired; María, dedicated almost exclusively to caring for him, is patient and affectionate, and sacrifices herself willingly to the grey and monotonous life he imposes on her. In the course of the play the profound love that each feels for the other is made evident. Manuel, José Luis's brother, who left home as a youth to seek his fortune outside of Spain, has just returned, wealthy and lonely, tired of working and traveling throughout the world. Instead of going to a hotel he decides to stay at his brother's house, seeking the warmth of a family. His optimistic, dynamic, happy, and attractive character is the very opposite of his brother's. He is well received. But from the very beginning the rancor and mistrust which had existed between the two brothers since childhood (particularly on the part of José Luis) is quite evident. María and Manuel like each other from the moment of their meeting. Manuel, with all his good intentions, is very friendly to María and showers her with attention and gifts. José Luis begins to feel upset and jealous.

The unmistakable affection which exists between husband and wife is reflected again and again in the dialogue. Yet, although it is never clearly expressed, nor do they seem to be aware of it, it may be surmised that a deep and potentially dangerous affection is growing up between Manuel and María. Each has qualities which the other needs. The tension mounts, and as María constantly praises Manuel's qualities, her now jealous husband becomes indignant and even provokes a tense scene with María. Everything is smoothed over immediately. Yet José Luis's distrust persists. At the end of the second act Benavente introduces melodramatic details. It appears that José Luis's hatred of his brother stems from the fact that he believes that Manuel is not his legitimate brother, but the son of a guardian of Manuel who, according to José Luis's suspicions, had seduced his mother. He is now afraid that Manuel will seduce María.

People begin to gossip. José Luis now considers his brother a dangerous intruder in his own home *(el nido ajeno)*. Manuel realizes all this and decides to leave. There is a violent argument between the two brothers in which José Luis's suspicions about his mother's honor are explained and dismissed. They bid each other farewell with an embrace. In the last brief scene, María, saying good-bye to Manuel, kisses him on the forehead. It is then that Manuel realizes that his brother was right, that he had been falling in love with María without realizing it. The play ends with these words:

> JOSÉ. *(Moved)* Good-bye, my brother. *(Embracing him.)*
> MARIA. Good-bye! But not forever . . .
> MANUEL. Forever, no! . . . Until we are very old and there is no longer room for mistrust and jealousy between us . . . When we can no longer doubt . . . not even ourselves . . . Then I will return to look for a corner to die in, in *el nido ajeno.*

The distinguishing characteristics of Benavente's theater are apparent even in this early play: psychological sublety, good dialogue, an adequate structure, a lack of exterior action, woman as the center of everything, love as a feeling which arises in spite of the characters' intention. The defects which recur throughout his work are also evident: expression of his own ideas through the words of the characters in long speeches which are more "literary" than dramatic; and his occasional tendency toward sentimentality and melodrama. In this case, however, everything is controlled and does not reach the extremes of other plays.

The action in the play is typical of Benavente. It demonstrates one of the outstanding characteristics of his themes and technique: the continual suggestion that something is going to happen which never happens. It is a continual stage game, with many moments in which it appears conflict will burst out into the open, the beginning of a strong dramatic tension which soon dissolves. Benavente retreats from conflict in this play as he does in many others *(Needles in the Mouth, The Thing to Do, Cousin Román, etc.)*.

At the time of the première of *The Intruder,* the public and the critics did not completely understand his new dramatic technique. The play did not arouse much interest, as audiences were accustomed to the plays of Echegaray and of Galdós. For this reason, the later revivals of *The Intruder,* when his theater had become established in Spain, were very successful. It was also very successful when, years later, it was performed in Italy.

The theme of the fickleness and inconstancy of feminine love, treated with irony and humor, appears in plays like *La escuela de las princesas (The School for Princesses),* with an aristocratic setting in an imaginary land. The King of Alfania and his ministers, for political reasons, want the Princess Constanza, the king's niece and heiress to the crown, to marry Prince Alberto, heir to the powerful kingdom of Suavia. But she is in love with the Duke Alejandro and wants to marry "for love." In the face of her refusal, the king and his ministers decide that it will be the Princess Felicidad, Constanza's sister, who will marry Prince Alberto, and Constanza will give up all her rights to the crown. All are satisfied and Constanza appears to be happy. The prince arrives for the wedding. He is intelligent and handsome, and when Constanza talks with him, she begins to regret her decision. Her love for Duke Alejandro grows cold and she feels strongly attracted to Prince Alberto. Toward the end of the second act, Benavente skillfully sets up a scene, between Constanza and the prince, which the audience has been awaiting. In it, Prince Alberto gives her a good lesson on happiness, duty and life. He says to her: "You have sought happiness too soon . . . little Princess with your crazy dreams . . . why didn't you wait?" Constanza, convinced that she has made a mistake, begins to flirt with the prince. In reality she only wants what she doesn't have and cannot get. Now she wants to marry Prince Alberto. A scandal follows in court. The king and his government don't want to change their plans, because the people agree with Constanza's first choice. In the end, Prince Alberto speaks seriously to Constanza of the duty and sacrifice which her position demands: ". . . happiness doesn't exist," he says, "but of all the appearances which cover up happiness, sacrifice is the most real." Princess Constanza, now reluctant, resigns herself to marrying Duke Alejandro.

The play takes place in an atmosphere of pleasant frivolity in which the merits of Benavente's dramatic art stand out clearly. The light, frivolous tone which almost reaches the level of a comic farce is also found in Benavente's eighteenth-century fili-gree *Amor de amar (In Love with Love),* a commentary on feminine coquetry. The setting is France of the eighteenth century. The Marquise Rosalinda is flirting unashamedly with three men at the same time: Lauro, a serious, rather philosophical man whose wife left him, running away with another man; the military man Rodrigo, direct, rough, and even brutal; and the Marquis Octavio, a lover of the Marquise Celia, Rosalinda's friend. Rosalinda plays at love with all of them in a joking manner without any of them ever really being important to her. The play ends with these words of Rosalinda: "My beloved is love . . . my love . . . is the love of love."

The play—dialogue, character and setting—is deliberately artificial. It is a play of pure dialogue, with little action: a very light bit of froth, rococo on stage. It is saved only by the charm and cleverness of Benavente's masterly dialogue.

El mal que nos hacen (The Evil They Do Us) is a play which is completely different in form and spirit from these others. In this play Benavente examines the problem of the man in love who does not know where to turn to find out the true feelings of woman, and the problem of authentic human communication in matters of love.

It concerns the plight of Germán, a man tormented and obsessed by woman's unfaithfulness. Quite rightly so. He was first deceived by his wife, whom he adored. Later, he was deceived by his mistress, who ran away with one of his friends. At the beginning of the play he lives with Valentina, although they are not married. Even though they appear to love each other, Germán is not happy, for he believes that Valentina, too, will deceive him. He particularly mistrusts Federico, a friend of hers from a poor family. He suspects that they were once sweethearts. Federico is certainly in love with Valentina, but has never said anything to her. Valentina, on her part, also suspects that Germán still sees his former mistress. This atmosphere of jealousy and mutual distrust becomes unbearable. Valentina and Germán have a conversation in which they speak clearly and with a profound psychological understanding of love between a man and a woman. In this conversation Germán makes a statement which may be considered a synthesis of Benavente's concept of feminine love: "The affection of a woman! Always unexplainable, and when it is most real, it is more uncertain than any lie."[7] Germán decides that it would be best to separate. Valentina is faint.

At the beginning of the third act she has left home to go to live in poverty with Federico and his mother. Germán is desperate, for he still loves her. He suffers a nervous breakdown. Valentina goes to see him, and their conversation concludes the play. Germán tells her that he cannot live without her and begs her to remain.

VALENTINA. Are we going to destroy another life? Do you also want me to hurt someone else as they hurt you and you hurt me? No, I can no longer be yours. I do not even belong to myself . . . Now I know that you love me as you have never loved me . . . Now that I shall be far away from you, you are more mine than you have ever been.

GERMAN. But you . . . will you never be mine? Never, never?

VALENTINA. In all your life, no one loved you as I did. Is not this being yours forever?

In spite of its defects—a clearly melodramatic sensationalism and a certain sentimentality of the sort Benavente often resorts to in plays where strong emotional conflicts appear—there are scenes of great psychological depth on the theme of love. The play's thesis may be summed up in one of Germán's statements at the end of the sixth scene of the first act: "If we are to accept the evil they do us we must understand that it is our punishment, punishment for evil we have done; we don't know how to comprehend that the evil which they do us without our having deserved it, the evil which we do to others who don't deserve it, is almost always punishment, the vengeance of evil which others have done." That is, evil is inevitable and is shared by all; we all deserve it because on our part we have done evil to one who didn't deserve it.

In these and in many of Benavente's other plays, one of his favorite themes is often repeated: the impossibility of achieving the happiness which man believes he can always find in what he doesn't have. There is, too, an ironic skepticism about love. As Leandro says to Crispín in *La ciudad alegre y confiada (The Happy and Confident City)*, "You know the heart of man, you know that passionate love is a fever which is only cured by one medicine: marriage."[8]

CHAPTER 6

Dramatic Technique

IN the use of technical methods and devices, the dramatist enjoys less freedom than either the poet or the writer of fiction. In the theater there are certain physical factors inherent in a play—the stage, the characters, the dialogue, its actual performance before the public, its division into acts, etc.—which determine its external structure. All are elements to which the playwright must inevitably submit, and it is his manipulation of them which constitutes dramatic technique as it is commonly understood.

Nevertheless, the term "technique" in literature is rather vague, as are most of those terms used in the discussion of art—content, form, realism, classicism, etc. Any attempt to analyze separately the formal elements of a work involves the danger of destroying, or at least of altering, its internal structure. Undoubtedly the technical elements must be viewed as elements fused with or integrated into the body of the work as a whole.

In this sense, "technique" is not simply the result of the manipulation of exterior or formal elements, but appears to be something substantive, something closely bound up in the whole process of artistic creation. In other words, artistic technique involves much more than the mere manipulation of formal elements. A change of technique implies a change of spirit, of sensibility, while conversely, a new artistic spirit or attitude demands a new technique. It was Flaubert who said that form rises from content as does heat from a fire. In other words, "form," in art, is an element which cannot be separated from "content." Indeed, form is a part of content.

In drama, particularly, questions of technique involve problems of theme and content. That is to say, they involve problems of *objectives*, of artistic goals, which reflect the complete "style," the personality and sensibility of the artist.

Benavente seems to have been in agreement with these views when he stated that ". . . dramatic cuisine is quite varied, all of it together constituting what we have agreed to call technique, which is the essential ingredient of the dish; whether it can be taught or learned, I don't know . . ."[1]

The new technique which Benavente introduced into the Spanish theater at the end of the nineteenth century reflected, then, a change of sensibility in relation to the existing theater. More concretely, it represented a change in sensibility in regard to the excesses of passion and the affectation of plot and gesture of the anachronistic romanticism of Echegaray. In general terms, the new theater of Benavente was characterized by its tone of natural conversation, the abscence of mannerism of gesture and emotion and the reduction of exterior action to a minimum.

I Dramatic Action

A study of Benavente's technique immediately reveals that the one thing which stands out most in the majority of his works is a weakened, at times almost non-existent plot conflict. This characteristic may be attributed to the playwright's conception of the dramatic art. All of the technical devices used by Benavente represent an orientation away from the portrayal of a dramatic conflict. Not only did such a conflict seem not to interest him, but he tended to eliminate it systematically.

When Benavente premièred his first two works, *The Intruder* (1894) and *Well-Known People* (1896), a large segment of the public and many of the critics were surprised at the lack of plot or action, in the traditional sense. In the beginning they failed to understand the new spirit and the correspondingly new technique which the author was introducing onto the Spanish stage. Because it was part of a convention so different from the traditional one which had reigned in the Spanish theater from Lope de Vega to Echegaray, it did not seem to them to be "theater" at all.

The playwright himself described the situation in a "self-critique" published in the newspaper *La Información,* October 22, 1896, the day following the première of *Well-Known People:*

The work was received with great pleasure; the public was greatly amused by that series of scenes which, in effect, *do not constitute a*

dramatic work. But the author did not intend it to be otherwise . . .
A strange thing happened last night; it was only when the play had
progressed almost to the fourth act that the audience felt that it had
been deceived, perhaps because then it understood that in these
scenes there might have been a real drama, and that the author,
capriciously, had been content to present only a sample. The public,
in general, was waiting for what is called a denouement. [My
italics]

Benavente was well aware of what he was doing, fully conscious of his artistic purpose. There is a certain irony in his
words when he says that the scenes of *Well-Known People* "do
not constitute a dramatic work," apparently referring to the differences between this work and the traditional concept of the
theater.

In *Well-Known People,* and in many other plays which he
wrote in the same style and which are most typical of Benavente, plot, or dramatic conflict, is secondary. Everything is oriented toward the dramatic incident; an incident which is the
implicit statement of its own essence. This new dramatic concept appears to emphasize the apparently nonessential, the mere
commentary or detail. Substance has been circumscribed, and
remains somewhat veiled. It is present, but only implicitly. It
is a matter of an essence, or content, which is more conceptual
than that of action. Here the action is internal, psychological;
it is more a matter of conflicting attitudes than of conflict overtly
expressed. Within the same or similar scenes the external action
could conceivably be very different, for it is secondary; what is
of most importance is the *intent* of that action.

The individual character, then, is frequently converted into
an instrument which enables the author to say what he himself
wishes to say. For this reason the characters often lack clear
individuality. Their consistency is more conceptual than vital.
They are characters constructed from without, characters which
grow out of the central idea of the play and are adapted to a
thesis. Their personality does not develop from a unique and
untransferable individuality in the midst of a whirlwind of feelings and passions. They are, above all, characters which form
a part of a milieu, of a particular social or moral climate. The
significant elements are precisely this milieu and the comments
expressed about it in the dialogue.

The main elements of the action, which almost always occurs offstage, are only a pretext for placing the characters in a particular dramatic situation. Action thus becomes a succession of atmosphere-creating scenes which convey the milieu; and the characters, particularly the minor ones, are more closely related to the scene of which they are a part than to the plot as a whole. What they say has a dramatic significance within that scene in the very moment they are speaking.. Thus in a very subtle way the author artistically fuses milieu and dialogue.

Within this dramatic formula the role of action has been reduced until frequently it dissolves itself in marginal ramifications. Incidents do not serve to emphasize a conflict or a character, but as dialectical brush strokes on the dramatic image as a whole. This dispersion, or decentralization, is only apparent. There is, without a doubt, a unity of concept, i.e., a thesis. Within it each character is marked by some definite psychological trait, not through his acts, but through what he says. He is consistent with himself and with the milieu of which he is a part. For this reason the true protagonist in these works is often a social group or a family rather than an individual. The characters are collective, and even when an individual stands out within the atmosphere which has been created, he always forms a part of it. Something similar occurs with a technique used by Galdós in some of his best novels (*Fortunata y Jacinta, Miau, El amigo manso*), although in Galdós there are always in addition strongly individualized characters.

Benavente's works may be considered a part of the *costumbrista* tradition, yet it is a *costumbrismo* very different from that of the Spanish novel of the nineteenth century. Benavente is not interested in the physical aspects of his dramatic images. He reflects and gives form to the subtleties of his characters' motivations and attitudes. His is a theater oriented toward the abstract. "Benavente's power," says J. G. Underhill, "of giving concrete form to the intangible and elusive qualities of human aspirations quickens the perception and thrills the imagination."[2]

This new concept of drama, with its appropriate technique, appears to have been perfectly defined from the beginning of his long career as a dramatist. This becomes evident in analyzing the characteristics of any of the first works which he wrote.

In *Well-Known People,* his second play, dramatic conflict is almost nonexistent, weakened to the point of only marginal significance. The author had at first titled it "Todo Madrid" ("All Madrid"). In a subtitle he classifies it as a play of "scenes of modern life," which is precisely what it is. There are many characters, twenty-two, to be exact, and each act is divided into brief scenes or images. The last act has seventeen of these.

Here is a résumé of the play: The family of the Duke of Garellano is going bankrupt and can no longer maintain before others the luxury and ostentation of former times. The mother, the widowed Duchess of Garellano, seemingly does not realize what is going on around her. Her son, Enrique, the present duke, is a "modern" young man, a cynical and unscrupulous playboy. He is interested only in money so that he can continue his life of diversion and maintain his position as a rich aristrocrat in Madrid society. The daughter, María Antonia, had a year before married Carlos, the Marquis of Vivares, himself almost bankrupt, a playboy and a cynic like the duke. María Antonia appears indifferent to the reckless life her husband is living.

At the beginning of the play she is very unhappy because she is going to have a child and the pregnancy is ruining her figure. Her brother, Enrique, is about to be married to Fernanda, daughter of the Count and Countess of Fondelvalle. Like the rest, it is a case of an arranged marriage, strictly a marriage of convenience. It is assumed that Fernanda will inherit the immense fortune of Hilario Montes, a businessman who with his money has managed to mingle with the aristocracy and who will be the best man at the wedding. Fernanda's mother, the Countess of Fondelvalle, has been the mistress of Montes, a fact known by everyone except her husband, and it is rightly thought that Fernanda is Montes' daughter. With the marriage of Enrique and Fernanda everyone's problem will be resolved. But Montes, who has an illegitimate daughter half-hidden away far from Madrid, decides to marry Petra Uriate, an audacious widow who has succeeded in gaining the confidence of Montes and his daughter.

Petra, meanwhile, has been Enrique's mistress. The Countess of Fondelvalle wants to prevent the wedding of Montes and

Petra because of jealousy and because such a marriage would destroy her plans. But it is the marriage of Fernanda and Enrique which is finally called off when everyone realizes that this marriage will no longer resolve anything. Petra then tries to arrange the marriage of her lover Enrique and her stepdaughter Angelita, but this young lady will not allow herself to be managed by anyone. She is serious, rational, and independent. She rebels against the low machinations of the others. She eventually comes to despise Petra, and when the duke attempts to court her she answers him with dignity, humiliates him and tells him never again to set foot in her house. Thus Angelita destroys the selfish plans of those who surround her. On this note the play ends.

The first brief scene soon clearly gives us the tone, the moral and social climate of the play. It is a dialogue between the duchess and her daughter María Antonia. We learn through their conversation of the projected marriage of the duke and the daughter of the Count of Fondelvalle. From this moment on the characters and the milieu are clearly established. The duchess appears naive and at the same time indifferent to the amorous intrigues of her children. María Antonia appears spoiled, ill-bred, gossipy and annoyed by everything and everybody. She is also indifferent to the disorderly life of her husband. Speaking contemptuously of him, her mother replies:

DUCHESS. Oh! Carlos is bad? So he has an evil character? Jealous? Mixed up in everything?

MARÍA ANTONIA. Well, he is, and he isn't. Really, he's a mere nothing, a common, ordinary fellow. And what good taste! Just look at his latest girlfriend!

DUTCHESS. Oh, who pays any attention to that! . . . It's only a lot of idle talk!

MARÍA ANTONIA. Just stop philosophizing about it. I've already told you I don't care a bit . . . But he could have better taste.

A little later, when María Antonia says something in bad taste about Petra, her mother replies with unconscious wit:

DUCHESS. You make me nervous the way you act. Such crude language! You frighten me when there are people around who might hear you, because you may be just as tactless in front of a respectable person as you are in front of me!

In spite of the slight and disperse action spread out over a multitude of scenes, commentaries, and incidents, the work does possess a unity of intent, of thesis. The central idea is clearly presented in the eighth scene at the end of the first act, in a conversation between Enrique and his mother:

ENRIQUE. I will not enter into a penniless marriage. I'm not about to put up with the humiliating life of a bankrupt aristocrat in my marriage. I can barely make out as a bachelor.

DUCHESS. Oh! You consider yourself a bankrupt aristocrat? What's wrong with the life you're leading now? Isn't it up to your position? What humiliations do you have to put up with?

ENRIQUE. It would take a long time to explain and you wouldn't understand me. In your day the aristocracy dazzled everyone with the splendor of its titles. Now anyone can carry a title; they are given away and sold for nothing, and if a person has money and knows how to spend it, no one is going to ask him where it comes from. You'll see Montes, once he's married to Petra, a very distinguished woman, directed by her, he will be more respected in all of Madrid than we are; his house will be a more distinguished social salon than ours is, and his daughter, that illegitimate daughter, heiress to an immense fortune, will marry . . . anyone she wishes, the most highborn, the most aristocratic . . . even me, if it's to my advantage!

This idea, that the old aristocracy, with its noble titles, must inevitably bow before the new aristocracy of money, before the dynamic and intelligent businessmen, is repeated throughout the work, implicitly and openly. In the fifth scene of the first act, the duchess, the duke, the Countess of Fondelvalle and her daughter Fernanda are talking. The Count of Fondelvalle is associated in important business matters with Montes. The Countess speaks:

COUNTESS. . . . in other times it would have been insulting to an aristocrat to refine sugar or to manufacture hard cider; but today . . . it's even the fashionable thing to do! You look at Montilla; they say he's making a fortune with his tomato preserves.

And in the second scene of the last act, at a grand party given in Montes' house, the same countess comments to Carlos, her husband:

COUNTESS. What dazzling luxury! Dear Carlos, now we might as well auction off our old relics. How could anyone receive visitors in her home after this! Our days are gone; let us bury the memory of them with dignity in our ancient mansion. We must yield to the new aristocracies of money and talent.

The late entrance of Angelita, in the final act of the play, has been considered a defect of the work, and some critics hold that she acts in a manner which is not consistent with her experience and education. I believe, however, that Angelita is in perfect accord with the central idea of the play. With this character the author gives greater force to his thesis. Among aristocrats, proud only of their name and their lineage, Angelita is the daughter of a common businessman, and moreover, an illegitimate daughter. Yet she appears as the only noble and dignified character in the entire work in the midst of counts, dukes and marquis who surround her. The intention is perfectly clear and in harmony with the thesis of the play.

When the play first opened, only *The Intruder* had previously been presented in public, and it had received a rather indifferent reception. For that reason it was not easy for Benavente to open *Well-Known People*. Both of the plays were presented in the *Teatro de la Comedia*, whose director, Emilio Mario, a friend of Benavente's family, accepted the play without great enthusiasm. Benavente read it beforehand in his home before a group of friends who customarily gathered in the *Cervecería Ibérica*. The reading of the play did not produce a very good impression. The dialogue was pleasing but everyone felt cheated by the lack of dramatic conflict. The actors themselves, when they gave the play, had a presentiment of failure.

The public, however, liked the play much more than was expected. Benavente's new formula was widely discussed. The jokes and ingenious sayings were repeated in the streets. Many people believed that they saw in certain characters allusions to "well-known people" of Madrid. The great interest which the play aroused suddenly converted Benavente into a famous playwright. It was with this work that he really initiated his ascendant career.

Benavente, in *Well-Known People,* and in many other plays in the same style, takes advantage of an artistic convention which is as licit and as justified as any other, as licit as that used by the Greek tragedians, by Shakespeare, Calderón or Lope de Vega. It is a convention which arises from a new way of conceiving the art of drama, which seeks, rather than action in itself, a reflection of that action in the characters' motivations. That which is reflected is oriented, by means of a dialogue which is always appropriate, toward the level of social satire. It is not an attempt to reflect Life, in capital letters, but of observing and commenting upon particular aspects, with narrower scope, of the life of a society. They are commentaries on the slack rope of human relations; they search out and find certain private motives of our actions which reveal important facets—usually weaknesses—of the human personality, all in a subtle and suggestive manner. J. G. Underhill states accurately that "the tendency of Benavente's art is away from the plastic toward the insubstantial, the transparent."[3]

And Azorín, answering the charge made against Benavente's theater that it lacks weight, affirms: "No, this lack is only apparent; what happens is that the center of gravity has been changed from one point to another. The work still has an intimate and solid organization but it is an organization very different from that of the traditional theater."[4] It is different precisely because the center of gravity has been changed from life seen as action and major conflict to the reflection of particular human problems as minor conflicts in a determined social context. What the characters say—what they think and want— is more important than what they do.

For this reason Benavente's theater has been classified as "literary." It is, undeniably, in the good and bad sense of the word. One can find in many of the dialogues a certain artificiality, a certain baroque quality in the psychological digressions, a certain exaggerated witticism. All of this, which is evident, does not detract from the dramatic value of his works. "Drama so subtle that it hovers continually among the shadows of the subliminal self might appear to be far divorced from the stage. Yet, in reality, Benavente is one of the most theatrical of writers."[5] Despite the lack of conflict, his works attained great dramatic interest in his time, as is clearly proven by the fact that he was the most popular and important dramatist in Spain for half a century.

In most of the plays of Benavente, despite appearances, there is little improvisation in their conception and planning, although often he wrote them very fast. He carefully planned the work from beginning to end. About this Benavente himself has written:

The dramatic work has different points of departure in its conception. Sometimes the author conceives an idea and for that idea seeks the characters who, because of their nature and their special situation, can best symbolize it. *In these works everything is subordinated to an idea. The characters go along as if the author guided them along tracks to reach the destination which he has set up for them.* [Italics added] At times, as in all works of art, the characters, through their own force, are more powerful than the preconceived idea and thus falsify or weaken it. What the play loses as an ideological work it will gain as a dramatic work. Again the point of departure may be the personality of one character, a miser, for instance, or an ambitious man. Other times the play has a point of departure a particular social milieu, or an historical epoch. In this case the background is more important than the characters, which must be held in subjection to the background, which is the true protagonist. In *The Witches' Sabbath* and in The *Bonds of Interest,* the first thing to appear was the principal idea of the work; afterwards the characters were the means of expressing it. In *The Lady of the House* the character of the protagonist was the important element, together with the environment in which the character could exteriorize itself with greater spontaniety . . . As works of mine in which the environment is the true protagonist I can cite for you *La inmaculada de los dolores (Our Immaculate Lady of Sorrows)* and *Well-Known People.* Nothing that happens in these plays could have happened in any other environment . . .[6]

In the majority of Benavente's plays, and above all in some of his best, "everything is subordinated to an idea" and "the characters go along as if the author guided them along tracks to reach the destination he has set up for them." They are thesis plays in which the characters are mere instruments designed to expound that thesis. Benavente, therefore, appears in such plays as a writer who thinks rather than as a creator of lives and worlds. Correspondingly, the technique is adapted to the artistic intent.

The technique reaches its perfection in the external structure of his works, in the scenic architecture. Through this external structure and a dialogue which is always skillful, ingenious and incisive, Benavente succeeds in producing works of great artistic value despite the fact that in them little or nothing happens. He prepares the scenes carefully, relates them to one another logically, moves the characters with consummate skill. Their entrances and exists on stage are always opportune. For that reason he does not need to give detailed stage directions in order to create the mood he seeks. The mood arises from the setting itself, created by the characters as they speak and move. He thus manages to give movement to the dramatic action, even though the latter may not have much importance. The result is an impression of naturalness and of ease of presentation.

The great number of characters which he presents on stage at times results in confusion when the work is read, but never when one sees it presented. "His theater is completely opposed to that of Galdós. The latter is more drama than theater; Benavente, on the other hand, is more theater than drama."[7]

II *Dialogue*

All the studies about Benavente coincide in affirming that he is a master of dialogue. In the first place, we may point out the extreme "facility" with which the characters of his plays speak. The dialogue flows with generous abundance, with no apparent effort. The author himself has said: "I write dialogue with great facility. The greatest labor is that of eliminating."[8]

The product of his labor is a flexible, fluid, ingenious, ironical, "elegant" dialogue, full of grace and delicacy. It can be compared to the best of Oscar Wilde or of Bernard Shaw. The spectator is charmed from the first moment by the conversation of the characters, which is at once polished and poignant; he is captivated by the abundance of sharp trusts and ironical comments. It is a dialogue, as I have already said, presenting more allusions and ideas than action; yet they are ideas which are always suggestive and fit perfectly into the atmosphere created on stage. It is an incisive, encompassing dialogue, one of ideas in continual gestation. J. G. Underhill notes accurately that "Benavente is not concerned with ideas, he is concerned with thought as it formulates itself, with ideas in the making."[9]

In the apparent dispersion of the action into scenes, it is the dialogue which lends cohesion of form and content to the work in an artistically achieved unity. This resultant unity is internal rather than external; that is, it is related not to the external structure of the dramatic intrigue, but to what can be called the substructure, the harmonious rhythm of words and thoughts. Benavente has said of it: ". . . all the art of dialogue lies in the rhythm. Dialogue without rhythm is dialogue without a soul. Words are the expression of what we think and feel. Our thought, like our heart, has a rhythm: sometimes accelerated, violent; other times leisurely, majestic. The perception of that interior rhythm is the secret of that art . . . Without a perfect musical sense—which is equivalent to saying an emotional sense—of words, it is not possible to be a dramatist."[10]

In this sense of rhythm, which preoccupied Benavente so greatly, it seems that he attempts to capture poetic quintessences. For that reason he speaks of the "musical sense," and a little further on makes the idea more concrete: "Music is the most sublime, the most divine art, because it is closest to that universal harmony of the spheres which Pythagoras came to perceive as the order and essence of all created things; the act of writing is a limitation, as is all labor . . . for that reason the best part of the work is not that which lies within it, but that which escapes from it."[11]

The rhythm, appropriate at all times, of Benaventine dialogue is one of its most outstanding characteristics. It is expressed in a careful, polished prose which in its best moments leaves in the spectator an impression of lightness, of fluidity, of deceitful facility. Whether or not he does manage with all this to capture poetic essence, as he doubtless intended, is another matter about which opinions differ considerably.[12]

The style of Benavente's dialogue is very difficult to imitate because the dramatic personality of the author is very vigorous. It causes a false impression of simplicity when, in fact, the style is very complex. It is a suggestive style in which the psychological undertone is the important element. Intention is implicit rather than expressed. In this is rooted the secret of his profound irony. It is a continual playing with the more or less hidden springs of our motivations and attitudes. The apparent inconsistency of many of our actions, on which Benavente insists, is revealed in subtle psychological probings which strip the souls of the characters. The author accomplishes this by pointing out the contrast between thought, intention, and words. Thus he brings us close to the falsehood and hypocrisy of man in society. ". . . the writer turns his characters about until we see all their facets at once, and at the same time we see them from within."[13]

With this continual play of words and intentions he reveals to us the personality of the character in an indirect, subtle and suggestive form. A single phrase tells us more about a character than all of the description of him. The characters are sketched in schematic form, consistent in their psychological revelation. He shows us the essential elements of their nature, that which is necessary to a particular stage situation. They are placed in very simple scenes, within which people merely converse, and apparently nothing happens.

In this sense, some of his best psychological works *(Pepa doncel, Nieve en mayo (Snow in May), The Evil They Do Us, The School for Princesses, 'n Love with Love,* etc.) become dramas of character as well as satirical and *costumbrista* dramas. The profile of the character is outlined in phrases full of ingenuity, humor, irony and psychological insight. The dialogues also reveal subtle facets of the character's personality.

Nevertheless, in the heart of the same positive qualities of the dialogue which give to many of his works great artistic and human value lie his principal defects, or rather, his excesses. Such excesses result from that same "facility" of which Benavente was so proud and which is so evident in his plays. It should be recalled that Benavente himself, speaking of this facility, added that "the greatest labor is that of eliminating." The dialogue springs up in irrepressible abundance from the mouths of the characters and it costs the author great effort to stem the overflow. The great ease with which Benavente makes his characters speak is frequently converted into a danger which he does not know how to avoid.

Benavente lets himself be carried away by his dangerous facility to the point of losing, on occasion, his sense of proportion. Then it appears as if the dialogue were converted into an end in itself. In many of his works—*La virtud sospechosa (Virtue is Suspect), Por las nubes (Among the Clouds), Los andrajos de la púrpura (Rags of the Royal Purple), Cuando los hijos de Eva no son los de Adán (When the Children of Eve Are Not the Children of Adam), El collar de estrellas (The Necklace of Stars)*, etc.—people talk much more than is necessary. These are works in which accessory conversation and trivial wordiness predominate. The conversation is ingenious, frequently subtle and always skillful, yet it is essentially marginal conversation which, for the most part, could be eliminated without the work's losing its meaning. On these occasions what little action there is, is diminished even further to the point of being drowned in words. The dialogue then attains substantive value to which everything else is subordinated.

The author is conscious of this danger and occasionally makes an effort to avoid it, but it costs him great labor. In some plays, as for example *Rags of the Royal Purple*, there are in the published edition many sections of dialogue marked with asterisks, and next to the list of characters, a note: "The paragraphs between asterisks can be eliminated in the stage representation." At times, also, he manages to maintain the interest of the spectator only by means of ingenious tricks, word plays, verbal subleties, ironic thrusts and jokes. The result of this is an intellectualized dialogue, cerebral and brilliant, but rather artificial.

Benavente usually speaks in these works, *El alfiler en la boca (Needles in the Mouth), In Love with Love, El rival de su mujer (His Wife's Rival), El demonio fue antes angel, (The Devil Was Once an Angel)*, etc. through the mouth of his characters. Many of them, as has already been indicated, are on stage to say things, to express ideas which the author wishes to say at any cost, even though they may have no relation with what is going on in the play. Even in these cases, the mastery of dialogue is so great that even though it is artificial and exaggeratedly witty, it does not, because, of its fluency and ease, lack a certain dramatic "naturalness."

In this way Benavente emphasizes his devastating irony. At the same time, however, some characters begin to lose individuality and to merge into the background. The author seems to be striving for a conceptual impact in his biting phrases. The spectator, however, accepts these witty characters with pleasure, and their words acquire a certain dramatic significance, because the ideas they express—usually harsh criticism with which he is in agreement—provoke his condescending smile and he soon comes to feel that he is actively participating in what is happening on stage. They are ideas which do not of themselves occur to the spectator, but once he hears them he considers them his own. Thus the play not only manages to hold his interest, but it also flatters him because it manages to make him feel more intelligent than he really is. The intention of the author and that of the public are then traveling the same road, in tacit and harmonious satiric collaboration. It is thus that the author achieves the effect he has sought in his use of dialogue. His technique, even when the objections already indicated are taken into consideration, remains completely valid and is fully justified within the framework of the play.

The quality of Benavente's style and technique ceases to be effective when sentiment and emotion come into play. In dramas like *The Evil They Do Us*, both the merits and the defects of his style exist side by side. While the story line is rather artificial and almost melodramatic, the dialogues stand out as valuable in themselves. They are very human and meaningful in their treatment of the complexity, paradox, and ambiguity of emotions like love, jealousy, mistrust, and hypocrisy. They show psychological depth and intellectual substance. Frequently, however, these dialogues do not fit in well with the artificiality of the events taking place on stage.

All this perhaps explains why Benavente, with great perceptiveness, tends to reduce action to the point of making it disappear in many of his works. The living, human consistency of the dialogues themselves is often lacking in the action. One is struck by the brilliance of a thoughtful, reflective dialogue which always shows a profound understanding of human nature. At the same time these plays point out the author's limitations in the creation of a fictional world and in the development of dramatic conflict. When he includes scenes dominated by sentiment or emotion, he tends to fall into long, rambling speeches which frequently border on sentimentalism, and even on bourgeois bathos. This happens, for example, in *Field of Ermine, The Necklace of Stars, La propia estimación (Self-Esteem)*, etc.

III   *Characters*

Indirect reference to Benavente's use of characters has already been made in the discussions of action and dialogue. Benavente is not a creator of great characters. The men and women who appear in his plays are not generally possessed of tragic greatness nor are they impelled by strong feelings. None of the characters imposes himself on our consciousness to the point of becoming the absolute center of action. Even in those cases in which the play does have a central character, the milieu is still just as important as the protagonist. With very few exceptions *(The Ill-Beloved, The Witches' Sabbath, The Noblewoman)* Benavente's theater systematically avoids violence, tragedy, the drama of strong passions.

In the plays which are centered around one character *(Princess Bebé, The Lady of the House, Little Man, The Angora Cat, The Governor's wife, Pepa Doncel, Mater Imperatrix)*, this is always a woman. The titles themselves refer unmistakably to the feminine protagonist. The same thing happens in other plays *Una señora (A Lady), Una pobre mujer (A Woman of the Poor), Al fin mujer (After All, a Woman), The Noblewoman* where the feminine character is of less importance. It could be said that all of Benavente's work is centered around the feminine soul. Masculine characters, without exception, are gray and shadowy, playing only secondary roles. The author appears to believe that the world, life, and above all society are in feminine hands.

Letters from Women (1893), his first important work and the one which first made him known, although it is not a work written for the theater, already evidences subtle shadings of feminine psychology. Benavente repeatedly expressed his strong inclination to deal with themes in which the feminine point of view predominates. He often spoke of his admiration for women, to which they responded in kind. He says, in this respect:

> . . . the admiration which is most welcome to me is that of the feminine public. This is undoubtedly just recompense for the affection with which I have always treated women in my works. In my long life I have had the good fortune, for it is good fortune, to have known very few women of whom it could be said that they were profoundly bad, and on the other hand, I have known many who are very good an also many who are admirable . . . [and about *Letters from Women* he adds:] Those letters proceed from the same feeling of affection and admiration for women which has inspired all of my work.[14]

The characters who have greatest individuality in his work are also women. As one who knew well the workings of feminine psychology, he drew women with more vigorous and vivid strokes than the men; their psychological profile is subtler and more profound. They are more "real." Masculine characters generally blend into a background dominated by a mother, wife or lover.

Mariano Alarcón says that the author has managed to attract the public with so great a power "simply by letting women talk." He adds that Benavente is a creator of "beautiful women." "In my opinion," he goes on, "it is his gift in this, his singular ability to create, to conjure up the souls of living women, that has won him the affection, respect and admiration of the Spanish-speaking peoples. All his women are absolutely individual and distinct. Each is different from every other. He has revealed woman to herself."[15]

The very opposite of Calderón in his treatment of the delicate theme of conjugal honor, he goes so far as to justify woman when she rebels against convention and social pressures as they affect marriage. Some of his works appeared very daring for the period in which they were written (*Little Man*, or *Another Kind of Honor*, for example). For Benavente, good and evil in human motivations are not clearly delimited. He justifies his bad characters, and his good characters are never completely virtuous. In his work there are neither heroes nor villains. In some plays, *The Devil Was Once an Angel*, for example, those who are supposed to be evildoers appear at the end to be better than the "good people." Particularly in the case of feminine characters, he always justifies their errors or bad qualities.

Because women are the center of his works, the actresses who have played in them have received more attention than the actors. Some of them—Carmen Cobeña, María Guerrero, Rosario Pino, Margarita Xirgu, Lola Membrives, Irene López Heredia, etc.—became well known and popular through their roles in Benavente's plays. Indeed, these great actresses contributed to a large extent to the success of many of his dramas. "You cannot remember my life as a dramatist," Benavente said, "without remembering Rosario Pino, the ideal interpreter of many of my plays."[16]

It is obvious that good actors contribute considerably to the success of any play. This happens to a more marked degree in the works of Benavente than in the plays of many other dramatists, for Benavente's plays need good actors to lend their personalities to the interpretation of characters who are, in themselves, rather formless and quickly become absorbed into the milieu of which they are a part.

CHAPTER 7

The Bonds of Interest

THE greatest virtues of Benavente's theater, simple structure, rapid action, polished, incisive dialogue, schematic characters, humor, and irony distinguish this play. The author's skeptical attitude toward the nobility of human motivation is very evident. The play has been classified, perhaps with exaggerated enthusiasm, as a "philosophical-moral satire", and it does encompass, within the limits set by its comical-satirical tone, the expression, even though to a minor degree, of a bitter and corrosively critical philosophy of social life.

I *Plot*

The play opens with an introductory prologue, written in excellent prose, which Crispín recites before the action begins. It is a beautiful and moving introduction to the drama to set its tone and purpose. Here we are told that the characters of the play are puppets, "the same grotesque masks of that Italian *commedia dell'arte,* but not as gay as they were, for in all this time they have thought a great deal."

The setting is an imaginary land at the beginning of the seventeenth century. The action develops directly, with no complications. The tone of farce is clearly established from the first dialogue. Leandro and Crispín have just arrived in the plaza of the city:

LEANDRO. This must be a great city, Crispin. One can see its greatness and wealth everywhere.

CRISPÍN. There are two cities. God grant that we are in the better one!

LEANDRO. Two cities, you say, Crispín? Now I understand, old and new, one on each side of the river.

CRISPÍN. What has the river, or oldness or newness to do with it? I say two cities, as there are everywhere in the world: one for those who arrive with money, and another for those who come like us.

Although well dressed, they are penniless and are fugitives from the law. Crispín takes the initiative from the very first, and advises Leandro on what they must do to win out in the city:

CRISPÍN. Here there is nothing to do but to make use of cleverness and shamelessness, for without shamelessness cleverness is worth nothing. What I have decided is that you must speak little and sharply, in order to give yourself the appearance of a person of quality; once in a while I will permit you to strike me. Answer mysteriously those who question you. And if you speak out of your own will, be sure that it is with dignity, as if you were pronouncing sentence. You are young and of fine presence. Up until now you have known only how to waste your talents; now is the time to take advantage of them. Put yourself in my hands. There is nothing so useful to a man as to have someone at his side to point out his merits, for modesty with oneself is foolishness; and self-praise, madness; and between them, the world is lost. We men are like merchandise; we are worth more or less according to the ability of the merchant who displays us.

They knock at the gate of an inn. Leandro is a bit frightened, but Crispín begins to lie and to resolve their first problems. He passes himself off as the servant of Leandro, who, according to Crispín, is a nobleman on an important mission in the city. He adds that their luggage is following them in eight carriages.

At this moment Arlequín, a poet, and *el Capitán,* a soldier, arrive at the inn. The innkeeper refuses to let them stay in the inn because they already owe him a lot of money. Crispín, in the name of his master, goes to their defense, flattering them shamelessly: "As a great lord, there is nothing greater in the world to him than a poet and soldier . . ." He adds that his master will gladly pay the expenses of both of them. The innkeeper then serves them dinner, and even lends them money. Leandro is increasingly frightened by the lies and trickery of Crispín:

LEANDRO. *(Aside to Crispín)* What madness is this, Crispín? How will we ever get out of this?

CRISPÍN. Just as we got in. Now you see; poetry and arms are ours. Onward! Let's go on to conquer the world!

In the following scene there appear Sirena, twice widowed and bankrupt, and Colombina, a former servant, young and pretty, whom Sirena has adopted as a daughter in the hopes of getting a good husband for her. But Colombina, to Sirena's displeasure, is in love with Arlequín. Sirena has arranged an elegant party for that same night, but the tailor, the caterers, the musicians, and the servants refuse to serve her unless they are paid in advance. Crispín finds out about all this, introduces himself to Colombina and tells her that he will arrange everything, providing that she and Sirena help him get Leandro married to Silvia, the beautiful daughter of the rich and powerful Polichinela; and that his master will know how to pay them well for their services. In the face of Crispín's daring, Colombina expresses her suspicions of him and of his master, and Crispín answers her with these words which touch on the essence of the play:

Never fear. Beside me you will find him the most courteous and attentive gentleman in the world. My shamelessness permits him to be modest. The hard necessities of life may force even the noblest gentleman to adopt the methods of the ruffian, as they sometimes force the noblest lady into the meanest position, and this mixture of villainy and nobility in the same person is out of harmony with the world. It is better to show as separate in two persons what is often confused and mixed together in one. My master and I, because we are one person, are each a part of the other. Would that it were always so! Each of us carries within him a great gentlemen of highest thoughts capable of all that is good and beautiful . . . And at his side the humble servant of the meanest tasks, he who must be engaged in the demeaning acts into which life forces him . . . The whole art, then, is in separating them in such a way that, when we fall into some villainy we can always say: It was not my fault. It was not I. It was my servant . . . You must already know who my master is: he of lofty thoughts and beautiful dreams. You must know, too, who I am: he of meanest acts, he who always grovels and toils on the ground in the depths of falsehood and humiliation and misery . . .

At that moment the musicians, servants, singers, the poets presided over by Arlequín, the soldiers with torches led by the

Captain arrive. Everything has been arranged by Crispín. Sirena appears, surprised, and Crispín speaks frankly to her, letting her know that he is aware of her past life. He gives her a document, a kind of contract, signed by Leandro, in which the latter promises to hand over to her a sum of money if everything comes out well; that is, if among them all they succeed in marrying Leandro to Silvia, the daughter of Polichinela. Sirena pretends to be indignant, but Crispín conquers her false resistance with facile words. The ball begins and during the evening everyone speaks admiringly of Leandro, the mysterious gentleman who becomes the center of attention.

Crispín, who had known Polichinela many years before when the two, condemned to the galleys, were in prison, speaks with him to remind him of his past. Cleverly, he forewarns Polichinela of the intentions of Leandro, who at this moment is dancing with Silvia. He tells him that he is a dangerous adventurer and that he should send Silvia away from Leandro, which Polichinela immediately does.

Leandro, who has sincerely fallen in love with Silvia, as has she with him, does not understand Crispín's strategy:

LEANDRO. You did that! What have I to expect now?

CRISPÍN. You are a fool. Well, that Polichinela will make every effort possible to see that you never again see his daughter.

LEANDRO. I don't understand!

CRISPÍN. This way he will become our strongest ally. It is enough that he is opposed to us to cause his wife to take the opposite side and for his daughter to fall even more madly in love with you. You don't know what a young girl, the daughter of a rich father, who has been given everything she ever wanted, is like when she, for the first time, finds someone opposing her will. I am sure that this very night, before the fiesta has ended, she will succeed in escaping her father's vigilance in order to talk to you.

Everything happens according to Crispín's plans. Silvia searches for Leandro and they meet in a dark corner. Sadly, they speak of their feelings. At this moment they hear the music which accompanies a song Arlequín is singing. At the same time Silvia recites the love poetry from the song as Leandro echoes it, repeating the last words.

[106]

The Bonds of Interest

They stand silently in each other's arms. Crispín approaches, and seeing them, says:

> Night, poetry, madness of lovers . . . !
> All must save us in this hour of need!
> Victory is certain! So courage and onward!
> Who else is the victor if love is ours!

As the second act begins Crispín spreads the news that Leandro has been attacked by men hired by Polichinela, who opposes Leandro's love for his daughter. The supposed attack was only a trick arranged by Crispín. All are alarmed and soon place themselves on the lovers' side. Silvia, unhappy, abandons her parents' house and goes to Sirena's, proclaiming that she will leave only to marry Leandro. Leandro, who no longer wants to keep up the pretense because he is sincerely in love with Silvia, refuses to go on lying and deceiving. But Crispín makes him see that now it is impossible to turn back, that the situation cannot continue as it is, for they have to pay the innkeeper, the owner of the mansion they live in, and the merchants who have given them credit. The scene ends with these words:

LEANDRO. But, how do we save ourselves? What can I do?
CRISPÍN. Nothing now. We can only accept what others have to offer us. We have become intimately involved in the interests of others and it is these bonds of interest which will save us.

Sirena arrives. She tells them that Polichinela knows who they really are; that he has proof of their none too admirable past life and that he has ordered the authorities to jail them. Now their only solution is for Leandro to marry Silvia. Leandro protests that he wants the truth known, whatever the consequences. Now Silvia, who has come with Sirena, appears, and Leandro tells her the truth: that he is only a miserable adventurer. She does not believe him. Then Polichinela, the innkeeper, Sir Pantaloon, the Doctor who represents the law together with his secretary, the Captain, Arlequín, and two constables come on stage. Silvia on seeing them arrive, has hidden herself. The scene which follows is very funny, indeed. The

Doctor wants immediately to begin the legal proceedings and to put everything in writing, making it clear that the complainants must pay a certain sum as a guarantee. The others pay no attention to him; the only thing they want is to recover their money. Soon a heated argument develops. But Crispín, with his logic, takes command and makes them understand that it is best to go on with the farce so that all may save their interests:

CRISPÍN. It is a fact that you are all interested in saving my master, in saving us for everyone's sake. All of you, so as not to lose your money; the Doctor, so as not to waste the vast store of doctrine he is amassing in those sarcophagi of learning; the Captain because everyone saw he was a friend of my master, and it is of greatest importance to his valor that there be no gossip about his friendship with an adventurer; you, Arlequín, because your poetic dithyrambs will lose all value if the evil purpose to which you put them is known; you, Polichinela, my old friend, because your daughter is already before Heaven and other men the wife of Leandro.

POLICHINELA. You lie! You lie! Insolent, shameless!

Then, Crispín draws back the drapery from the rear door and Silvia, Leandro, Sirena, Colombina, and Polichinela's wife appear together in a group. Polichinela is indignant. He declares that everyone has conspired to rob him, and wants Leandro taken prisoner. Leandro declares that Silvia should be taken away before he himself is turned over to the authorities. Silvia defends him:

SILVIA. Father! If you do not save him, I will die. I love him. I'll always love him, now more than ever, because his heart is noble and he was very unhappy, and he could have made me his by lying and he has not lied.

Then everyone speaks enthusiastically in favor of the wedding. Polichinela threatens to disinherit Silvia and leave her without a dowry. Leandro and Silvia answer that money is of no importance to them. Everyone else thinks they are mad. At last, Polichinela reluctantly agrees under pressure from all those who are present. The play ends with these words:

CRISPÍN.   . . . What did I tell you, my lord? That among them all they would save us . . . Believe me. If you would get ahead in everything in the world, the bonds of love and affection are as nothing compared to the bonds of interest.

LEANDRO. You are mistaken, for without Silvia's love I would never have saved myself.

CRISPÍN. And is there not a great bond of interest in this love? I have always realized the part the ideal plays, and I have always counted on it. But now the farce is ended.

SILVIA. *(To the audience.)* And in it you have seen these little puppets, like human beings in the farces of our lives, moved by those now gross, now delicate strings which are their interests, their passions, their illusions, and all the misery of their condition. Some are pulled by their feet and carried off on sad and endless wanderings; others, by their hands to labor with pain, struggle with rage, rob with cunning, kill with violence. But among all of them, there descends at times a thread so delicate and fine that it seems woven of the light of the sun and the moon: the thread of love, which makes human beings seem divine, and brings to our brow the splendid light of dawn, and gives wings to our heart, and tells us that not everything in a farce is farce, that there is something in our life which is true and eternal and which cannot end when the farce ends.

II *The Play's Thesis*

Through this résumé of the plot, only a pale reflection of the play itself, it can be clearly seen that the drama is based on one thesis or central theme: the power which the bonds of interest have on our motives and acts. Law, honor, and dignity bow before such interests, changing our life in society into a series of acts dominated by hypocrisy and deceit.

This thesis is in accordance with the author's skeptical philosophy which is presented, implicitly or explicitly, in many of his plays. In this sphere Benavente's sharply satirical attitude is unfolded in his many social satires which are but variations on the same theme.

For this reason, *The Bonds of Interest* may be considered the most representative play of Benavente's theater. Even the happy ending, where it appears that only love is saved, is one of the author's ways of leaving a hopeful and optimistic note in the spectator's mind. But it also appears that Benavente only half believed in love and happiness. As he says, in the words of the protagonist of *Princess Bebé:* "Happiness doesn't exist. There are only happy moments." Nine years later, in 1916, he premièred *The Happy and Confident City,* the sequel to *The Bonds of Interest.* The same characters appear. In this second play Leandro, now married to Silvia, sets out to seek adventure with other women. It is then that Leandro tells Crispín: "You know the heart of a man; you know that passionate love is a fever that is only cured with one medicine: marriage." *The Happy and Confident City,* in spite of the great success and the controversy that it aroused (due above all the political and patriotic interpretations of its content), is greatly inferior to *The Bonds of Interest.* It lacks the charm, freshness, irony and spontaneity of this play.

III *Characters*

The characters of *The Bonds of Interest* are schematic, and for this reason somewhat rigid. The author intended to create such characters, and the result is effective. In the prologue Benavente wrote:

This is a puppet play, on an impossible theme, with no reality at all. You will soon see how the things that happen in it never could happen, that the characters are not men and women but puppets and marionettes of cardboard and cloth, with strings which are visible even in little light and to the most near-sighted.

As has already been pointed out, the characters of Benavente's plays often lack individuality. Their human quality is only a reflection, more conceptual than vital. In *The Bonds of Interest,* a thesis play, a play of ideas, this is not a defect but one of the play's greatest virtues. The characters are generic types, representative symbols. All, in their complex coexistence with others, wear the mask which circumstances impose on them. In other words, each plays his part in the comedy of life, which in this case is the dual farce of the play: Leandro and Crispín, penniless adventurers fleeing from the law, pass themselves off as a powerful nobleman and his servant, and when Leandro wants to appear as he really is, he cannot; the Captain and Arlequín are the incarnation of the ambiguous and sad role of the unsuccessful hero and poet; Sirena, bankrupt, who gives grand balls to maintain her social position, sees herself forced to act with the shamelessness of a Celestina; Colombina, the former servant, passes herself off as Sirena's niece; Polichinela, once a thief, murderer, and galley prisoner, is now rich and respected in the city. Silvia, who represents innocence, candor and ingenuousness, is the only important character who appears without a disguise.

The central character who moves the threads of the action is Crispín. He was the author's favorite character, and Benavente himself often played the role on stage.

Leandro and Crispín may be interpreted as two, apparently paradoxical, aspects of human personality. Benavente states this clearly in the words of Crispín: "My master and I, because we are one person, are each a part of the other." This is an interpretation parallel to that which has repeatedly been made of the central characters of the *Quijote;* but this does not imply any comparison between the two works nor their characters.

The Bonds of Interest is a play of great perfection, with a fully realized sense of unity. The dialogue flows naturally and concisely, closely integrated with the action which leads directly to the climax. It is one of Benavente's plays in which his qualities as a dramatist are most in evidence. It is a masterpiece. Together with *The Ill-Beloved,* it is Benavente's drama which has enjoyed most success in Spain and abroad.

CHAPTER 8

The Witches' Sabbath

THIS is perhaps Benavente's most ambitious play. In it he combines the multiple facets of his dramatic talent in a complex and original synthesis. Well aware that he goes far beyond the limits of traditional theater, the author calls it a "dramatized novel in five acts." His was a shrewd observation, for the theme, content, and development belong as much to the novel as to the theater; yet, Benavente succeeds in enclosing the novelistic dispersion of the drama into a dialogue and a structure that turn it into a vigorous play with lyrical, philosophical, and dramatic ramifications.

The play is preceded by a poetical prologue in which Benavente gives us an interpretative synthesis which is at the same time a masterful example of the creation of atmosphere. The action unfolds in an imaginary time and place, on the "witches' sabbath," any bewitched moment of life in which mad fantasy and crude reality are mixed up in a confusing vortex; the place, "a corner of the earth enchanted by nature," located, as indicated at the end of the cast of characters, in "a winter resort somewhere between France and Italy." In this corner of the world a group of human beings of all social levels is anxiously searching for their "paradise on earth." The setting is ideal, for it could be the sought-after paradise, but these men flee from cold and bring the coldness of their life with them; they flee from life and their life follows them . . . For them, every road is like a Dantesque hell, and thus it can be said on their entrance,

> I am the way into the city of woe.
> I am the way to a forsaken people.
> I am the way into eternal sorrow.

The Witches' Sabbath

The allegorical, symbolical tone of the drama is established by these lines from Dante's *Divina Commedia* quoted in the prologue. The whole play acquires meaning if we take into account the metaphor of the prologue. In this atmosphere, the characters do not need to be "of flesh and blood," or individualized, for they are part of a sustained allegory. The princes, aristocrats, adventurers, circus performers, policemen, women from the heights and depths of the world are puppets in a great farce which develops simultaneously in luxurious palaces and in the most sordid taverns. It is a play of strong contrasts in which the author presents us with an amorphous conglomeration of satire, humor, tragedy, and fantasy; reflections on the ideal, on art, love, and death; all done in a manner bordering on both reality and fantasy.

The first act is typical of the genre of light, sophisticated satire on high society which Benavente handles with such skill. It is reminiscent of scenes of *Well-Known People*. The setting is the hall of a sumptous villa, where the author brings the ten characters together in the following manner:

> Edith is playing a lute, Lady Seymour and Leonardo are listening to the music; Princess Etelvina, Prince Miguel, Lord Seymour and the Duke of Suavia are having tea in another group; Prince Florencio, Countess Rinaldi, and Harry Lucenti are leafing through engravings and talking excitedly. Various servants are waiting on them. A servant hands a telegram to Prince Miguel.

The development of this scene, with its obvious tone of elegant affectation, is masterfully executed by the control, based solely on the dialogue, which Benavente always shows in this kind of situation. The characters talk with those in their group and occasionally with others. The dialogue is a pointed satire on human weakness and hypocrisy.

The telegram which Prince Miguel has just received reveals that the Emperor of Suavia has just had a son, an heir to the throne. Until then, the heir was Prince Florencio, a young playboy concerned only with enjoying himself; and next in line, his uncle, Prince Miguel. The Emperor of Suavia had sent them far away from his court so that they would not become too impatient to inherit the throne. But Prince Florencio and his uncle consider the crown a heavy and bothersome burden and are quite content with the pompous, useless, and irresponsible life they are leading.

At the beginning of the last scene of the first act, the play's most important character, Imperia, appears. She is the mistress of Prince Miguel, a weak man whom she dominates completely; and before that, she was the mistress of his nephew, Prince Florencio, who met her in the study of the artist Leonardo, where she was working as a model. From a very poor family, Imperia had once been a dancer who was at times forced to beg in order to eat. At that time her name was Donina. Leonardo took her away to his house, giving her father 500 lira. Imperia has a daughter, also called Donina, whose father is in jail, serving a life sentence because he murdered a foreigner while robbing him. Imperia says that he is the only man she has loved and she still loves him. Imperia's daughter now works in a circus. Imperia goes to see her every night. Donina is fourteen and is madly in love with Nunú, a circus rogue who pays her no attention.

There is an extreme contrast between the characters of the play: on the one hand, princes and aristocrats; and on the other, people from the lowest levels of society, circus artists and adventurers. The author clearly shows that no one is better than anyone else. When Imperia tells Prince Miguel the details of her life, he replies that all that seems horrible to him. She answers:

. . . Yes, and how is it among you, eh? Where is your affection? You don't insult each other, certainly, you don't go around hitting one another, nor does anyone give 500 lira when he falls in love or marries one of your women. It's just that among you nothing seems to be what it is. Not what you feel, nor what you say . . . And among us, everything is real, so it seems much worse.

The second act, in strong contrast to the first, takes place in Mr. Jacob's circus, a popular gathering place. In the waiting room there appear a half-drunk elephant trainer, a clown, and a few prostitutes. Prince Florencio and Harry Lucenti, a writer who acts as the Prince's secretary and who arranges his orgies, arrive. Florencio wants them to arrange something for him tonight which is "really great and devilish," this with the attendance of Donina, to whom he is now attracted. The prince speaks to Nunú and gives him valuable gifts so that he will bring Donina to the party. At this moment Imperia and Donina, and a little later Countess Rinaldi and Leonardo, come on stage. Now everyone is together, the "high" and the "low," yet in an atmosphere where the hypocrisy of the elegant salon has disappeared. Countess Rinaldi, who is the acrobat's mistress and who wants to go into business with the elephant trainer, comments:

Here, more or less, we are all the same. We can greet each other and speak frankly, although tomorrow it will seem as if we have never seen each other.
Imperia replies: "It is our *almas brujas* (witches' souls) which greet one another . . ."

Continuing, Imperia expresses an idea which synthesizes the play's meaning:

IMPERIA. Among many peaceful hours of life there is for all of us a night when our *almas brujas* fly off to their witches' sabbath. We live through many indifferent hours for this one hour which interests us. One hundred souls fly off, some toward their dreams, others toward vice, others toward love; toward what is far from our life, and yet is our life.
RINALDI: It's true. We are in our witches' sabbath. We may greet each other. Greetings, my sister!
IMPERIA. Greetings, my brother! Where are you flying? Toward good or toward evil?
LEONARDO. I? To where life disappears, as in a dream.
RINALDI. I? To the kingdom of love, where death never enters.
LEONARDO. And you, Imperia, what are you looking for?
IMPERIA. I am looking for myself. I am looking for Donina, poor, ignorant, and in love. Your art revealed to me the beauty that I possessed, and because of it I will get what I dream of.
LEONARDO. What is that?
IMPERIA. Treasure, treasure! Money is the great force, with it you can get anything: good or evil, justice or vengeance.

When Imperia discovers that during the party which they have planned for that night, Nunú is going to sell Donina, handing her over to Prince Florencio, she decides to attend, too, in order to prevent it. Thus the second act ends. All is ready for the witches' sabbath.

The third act takes place in a tavern full of sailors and bums, where Prince Florencio has arranged his orgy. It is here that there appears a secondary, but important, character, Maestá, an old drunk who tells the story of her life:

> Well, I was pretty once, and portraits of my face and statutes of my body stand guard in palaces and museums . . . Very great, powerful, and wise men have loved me . . . Even a king, who with one word from me would have given up his crown. You see me now? Well, I have worn on my body dresses embroidered with pearls worth a kingdom. In the flower of my youth I spent in one day what I would only want now for the rest of my life . . .

When Imperia enters, one of the group asks Maestá: "Don't you know that queen?" Maestá answers: "A queen? Wasn't I a queen? No, I don't know her."

Prince Florencio, Donina, Nunú, and other guests at the party are inside in another room. They tell the prince that Imperia is in the tavern, and he invites her to come in. At that moment, when Imperia turns to go into the room where the party is being held, shouts are heard. Prince Florencio appears at the door bloody and dying, leaning on those who are with him. Donina, when she discovered what they had plotted against her, had stabbed the Prince with a dagger. Hearing the commotion, the police arrive. There follows a scene of great dramatic force. They place the now-dead prince in the middle of the group as if he were drunk. They have washed off the blood with the contents of a bottle, and everyone begins to sing and dance around him. The police, looking in on the scene, don't suspect what has happened and leave. Imperia decides to take the body to her house.

The fourth act takes place in "a room of Imperia's villa." Prince Florencio's body is hidden in her house. The police prefect and Prince Miguel arrive, looking for the prince. Imperia tells them the truth about what has happened, but adds that it would be best for everyone to hide the real facts by saying that he committed suicide. If the truth becomes known

in Suavia about the life of vice that Prince Florencio was leading and that Imperia is Prince Miguel's mistress, everyone will
be in trouble. Much more now that, because of the death of
Prince Florencio and of the emperor's son (news that has just
arrived from Suavia), Prince Miguel is the heir to the throne.
Imperia convinces them of the necessity of hiding the truth.
She intends to destroy reality and believes that by wishing it
away it will flee like a ghost. But in the next room is Princess
Etelvina, Florencio's mother, who is heard crying. Donina has
also arrived. Imperia, confused, says:

I can't go on! . . . They weren't ghosts, reality can't be destroyed!
It comes into our lives, and it destroys us . . . That mother who
weeps for her child, my daughter who is dying of fear and sorrow,
they seize my heart and they destroy it!

The fifth and last act takes place in the garden of Imperia's
villa. Donina, after all that has happened, is very ill. Imperia
forces Nunú to stay with them and pretend he loves Donina,
threatening to accuse him of complicity in Prince Florencio's
death. But Nunú has for some time been unable to pretend.
Donina at last discovers Nunú's real feelings, and the shock
places her near death. At this time Prince Miguel is waiting for
Imperia in order to sail in his yacht to Suavia to be proclaimed
emperor. Donina dies. Imperia overcomes her sorrow when
she sees that her life-long ambition is being accomplished, and
goes away with Prince Miguel to be Empress of Suavia. As the
play ends, Imperia says:

To realize something great in life one must destroy reality; one
must get away from the ghosts which bar our path; one must follow,
as the only reality, the path of our dreams toward the ideal, where
our souls fly on their witches' sabbath, some toward evil, to be lost
in it like spirits in the darkness; others toward good, to live eternally
among the spirits of light and love.

It should again be pointed out that the play is an allegory.
Does Imperia succeed in destroying reality? Only for a moment, and only in her imagination. Of the three feminine characters, Donina, Imperia and Maestá, reality is incarnated in

Donina, who dies of sorrow, and in Maestá, the old, half-mad alcoholic. Imperia, as the play ends, still lives in a world of illusion, she still believes it possible to destroy reality. Donina, who succumbs because of an excess of feeling, represents one aspect of Imperia's personality, the past. Maestá, old and destroyed, is the future which probably awaits her. Imperia, in her attempt to reach her ambition of power, dominion, and wealth beyond reality, suceeds in appearance only. Crude reality is triumphant. Even if she realizes her dream, it is paled by the tragic hues of reality. The price of her dream is too high for her momentary triumph to be satisfactory. In essence she is more unfortunate now than in the past, represented by Donina, or in the future, symbolized by Maestá.

In *The Witches' Sabbath* Benavente gives free rein to his imagination in combining his best qualities: delicate irony, biting satire, humor, and an intellectualized dialogue with penetrating observations on life, happiness, sorrow, art, love, the will to dominate, death . . . It is all expressed through characters who search for meaning in life, who futilely seek happiness in many ways: Imperia, with her ambition; Prince Florencio, in his vices; Prince Miguel, subordinating his will to Imperia's; the artist Leonardo, in pursuit of elusive beauty; Donina, carried away by her heart; Countess Rinaldi, in the extravagance of the neurotic woman; and Maestá, now defeated, through the oblivion of alcohol. All are frustrated, defeated beings. Only Imperia seems to triumph over all, yet the shadow of Maestá falls over the future.

In this play, Benavente resolves the fusion of two genres: the novel and the drama, in harmonious unity. There are inevitably rather wordy explanatory passages where the novel is most in evidence (for example, in the second act, where Leonardo tells Countess Rinaldi of his relations with Imperia, how he made a statue of her, and his flight with Prince Florencio). Yet, Benavente's dramatic technique dominates everything. The result is an original play of vast scope which is one of Benavente's best works.

CHAPTER 9

Rural Plays

BENAVENTE wrote two plays with an authentic rural atmosphere, *The Lady of the House* and *The Ill-Beloved.* A third play, *The Noblewoman,* may also be included in this group although there are several characters from the city in it. The setting of the three plays is "a small town of Castile."

The author had a country house in Aldeaencabo, a small village in the province of Toledo, where he would go to rest, far away from the hectic life of Madrid. There he meditated, wrote, and was able to be alone, something he always liked very much. He would take long walks in the neighborhood, speaking to no one. In Aldeaencabo he met a woman married to the village Don Juan, who was the inspiration for his character of Dominica in *The Lady of the House,* as he himself tells us. This was his first play with a rural setting.

Yet this atmosphere never attracted him. According to Ismael Sánchez Estevan,[1] he wrote his second rural play, *The Ill-Beloved,* as the result of a compromise. He needed a new play for the theatrical company of María Guerrero, and had thought of giving them *The Necklace of Stars,* which he was then writing. But he wanted the great actress María Guerrero to be able to display her exceptional dramatic talent, and as in this play she would have had the part of an elderly servant, he decided to write a play of strong emotions especially for her, "giving free rein to the dramatic vein so that our great tragedienne may display her astounding faculties." As María Guerrero's theatrical company urgently needed the play, he wrote *The Ill-Beloved* very rapidly, "a toda máquina" in Benavente's words, and as on other occasions when he wrote for a deadline he handed it to the actors act by act. Because this drama is the best of the three plays with a rural setting, it is convenient to discuss it first.

I   *The Ill-Beloved*

The action takes place in a small Castilian town, among rather well-to-do peasants. The main characters are a married couple, Raimunda and her second husband Esteban, and Acacia, Raimunda's daughter from her first marriage, who lives with them.

In the first scene, friends and neighbors have gathered in the home to congratulate the family on Acacia's engagement to Faustino, a young peasant from a neighboring town. Acacia had had another suitor, Norberto, with whom she had broken off for reasons which do not seem clear at this time.

Acacia, reserved and shy, seems to have accepted her marriage to Faustino without enthusiasm. When all visitors have left, her mother asks her:

RAIMUNDA. . . . What have you to say, child? Are you happy?
ACACIA. You can see for yourself.
RAIMUNDA. You can see for yourself! Well, that's what I'd like, to see for myself! Who knows what's wrong with you!
ACACIA. I'm just tired.

It is after nightfall when Faustino and his father ride back toward their village. Esteban accompanies them to the outskirts. Someone hidden in the thicket, shoots and kills Faustino. It is said that it was Norberto, Acacia's onetime suitor. Here the first act of very rapid action ends. Faustino's death injects a tense note of mystery just as the curtain falls.

As the second act begins, Esteban's family have gone to spend a few days at a nearby house in the country, fleeing from the gossip of the people. Norberto has been able to show that he was far away when the murder occurred, and after a few days in jail, he is set free. But Faustino's father and brothers are convinced that Norberto is guilty and want to seek revenge. The tension grows.

Raimunda, in order to find out the truth, calls Norberto and has a talk with him in her country home. In reponse to her questions, Norberto says that he had broken off the engagement with Acacia because he was afraid. He names El Rubio, Este-

ban's servant, as Faustino's murder; but it was Esteban who
incited him to act as he did. Norberto states that El Rubio is
now spending a great deal of money which he has undoubtedly
received from Esteban. Drunk in the tavern, El Rubio has told
much of his tale. Norberto adds that many suspect that Esteban,
in love with Acacia, doesn't want her to marry anyone. He then
tells Raimunda that in the town they are singing a little song in
which the reason for the murder is maliciously implied:

> He who loves the Soto girl
> must be tired of living.
> Because of the one who loves her
> they call her the ill-beloved.

Raimunda, discovering the truth, which she had not suspected,
is overcome. Then Norberto leaves. While he has been talking
with Raimunda, Faustino's brothers are waiting in the fields to
kill him. The second act ends with a violent scene in which
Raimunda accuses Esteban of being a coward and a murderer.

At the beginning of the third act, Norberto has been wounded
by Faustino's brothers and has taken refuge in Raimunda's house.
Esteban and El Rubio have fled and are hiding in the fields,
fearful because of the turn of events. Then they return, Esteban
having decided to surrender to the police. But Raimunda, who
still loves Esteban in spite of everything, pardons him and advises him that it would be best not to say anything in order to
see if, in time, everything will work out all right. Esteban
weeps and Raimunda talks to him as if he were a child:

RAIMUNDA. . . . Don't cry, don't hide your face, you have to lift
up your head, as I do when they come to question all of us. See to
it that they don't see the smoke even if the house is burning. Dry
your eyes; they must have wept tears of blood. Drink a glass of
water. It should be poison for you. Don't drink so quickly, you're
all sweaty. Look how you've come back all scratched up by the
brambles! They must have been knives! Come, let me wash you,
you look a fright!

Raimunda, with a woman's sense of the practical, is determined above all else to save her family. She suggests that it is
best to get Acacia away from home, to send her to distant rela-
tives. There, in time, everything will be forgotten and she can

marry. But Acacia, who has overheard the conversation from the next room rebels, saying that she will not go away:

ACACIA. You won't get away with what you want to do. If you want to save this man and keep everything which has happened here quiet, I will tell the police and everyone. I don't have to look out for anything except my own honor; not for the honor of someone who has none, has never had honor, because he is a criminal.

RAIMUNDA. Be quiet, my daughter, be quiet! It gives me chills to hear you talk that way. So you hate him, when I have almost forgiven him!

ACACIA. Yes, I hate him, I've always hated him, and he knows it, too. And if he doesn't want to see me denounce him, let him come kill me. Yes, I'd like that, for him to kill me. Yes, let him kill me, to see if for once you would stop loving him!

RAIMUNDA. Hush, hush, child.

At this point Esteban enters, and the play's last brief scene unfolds. It is here that Acacia's real feelings, hidden until then, are revealed. It is a scene of violent and tragic intensity. Acacia has never called Esteban "Father." Raimunda wants to compel her to do it:

RAIMUNDA. Won't you call him father, my child?

ESTEBAN. She will never forgive me.

RAIMUNDA. Go on, child. Embrace him. Let him hear you call him father. Then even the dead will forgive us and rejoice with us!

ESTEBAN. My daughter!

ACACIA. Esteban, oh God, Esteban!

RAIMUNDA. You still don't call him father? Have you lost your mind? Oh, mouth to mouth in her embrace! Get away, get away, now I see why you wouldn't call him father! Now I see that it is you who is to blame for everything. I curse you.

ACACIA. Yes, yes! Kill me! It's true, it's true! He's the only man I've ever loved.

In the fact of Acacia's actions and words, everyone loses his head. Esteban tells Acacia that they will run away alone, and that he will protect her against everyone. Raimunda, desperate, shouts for the neighbors and tries forcibly to stop Esteban from leaving the house. Esteban fires the shotgun and mortally wounds Raimunda. The tragedy ends with Raimunda's words to Acacia:

RAIMUNDA. That man no longer has any power over you! You are saved. Blessed be this blood which offers salvation, like the blood of Our Lord!

The ending has a certain aura of Greek tragedy about it in the sacrifice of the innocent to uncontrollable forces of life, to destiny. Yet there are certain facets of the characters' reactions which affect and rather distort the action in which the hand of the author, who only intended to provoke the last outburst, is too evident. Raimunda's insistence that Acacia and Esteban come closer and embrace, when she is aware of Esteban's violent love for Acacia, is not very convincing. It also seems strange that Raimunda would never have suspected what was going on in her own house, before her very eyes. We should think that her intuition might have made her aware of these feelings no matter how much they tried to hide them.

Of the three main characters, the most complex and interesting is Acacia, with her mixture of hate and love toward Esteban. Esteban's character is gray and shadowy, as always happens to men in Benavente's plays, where, without exception, feminine characters are the more sharply defined.

In this play and in *The Lady of the House,* Benavente imitates the language of the people of the village in an effort to give more local color. His imitation, however, is somewhat affected and conventional, not quite authentic, as most critics have observed.

There is also in *The Ill-Beloved* a certain aura of the detective play in the development and resolution of the main problems: that of who killed Faustino, which is solved at the end of the second act; then there is the mystery of Acacia's true feelings, a mystery only cleared up at the end of the play. The whole play has been constructed around the last scene with great technical skill, although with certain faults, as we have indicated. The structure is oriented toward a clearly melodramatic effect reminiscent of Echegaray. In this sense the first two acts are much superior to the last, which is too exclusively oriented toward the explosive effect of the last scene.

Yet, perhaps because of the melodramatic sensationalism which always pleases the mass audience, it has been Benavente's most successful work, both in Spain and abroad. J. G. Underhill's translation of the play, called *The Passion Flower* was first performed in the Greenwich Village Theater in New York, January 30, 1920, with success. In 1923 it had already been performed more than 750 times in different theaters throughout this country. It also was made into a movie in Spain and Mexico.

II *The Noblewoman*

Melodramatic sensationalism reaches its extreme in *The Noblewoman*. The setting is also a small village of Castile. The characters, however, belong to two very different social classes: the gentlemen who own the land and who go to the country only to spend periods of rest and to look over their estates; and poor peasants who, as servants, work on and care for their landlords' lands and houses. Only in part may it be considered a rural play.

The plot is as follows: A peasant couple, Martín and Marciana, carefully work the estate of a wealthy family from Madrid. Their daughter Pilar and José María, a young man they took as a child and have reared as a son, live with them. José María is really the son of doña Isabel, the unmarried lady who is the owner of the manor house in which the action takes place. Martín, Marciana, and many people of the town believe that his father was Marciana's brother, also a peasant and servant in the house, who was murdered by Leoncio, doña Isabel's brother, to prevent him from marrying Isabel. Leoncio, a very dominating and ambitious man, blamed the death on some clandestine hunters whom no one saw, but everyone suspects the truth. Pilar and José María, although brought up as brother and sister, suspect that they are not. Later, José María learns that his mother is doña Isabel and also believes that his father was Marciana's brother.

As the play begins, doña Isabel has returned to her country house after an absence of twenty years; it was twenty years ago that the murder was committed. Her brothers, Leoncio and don Rafael, also single, are about to arrive. Don Rafael is a

weak man, sickly and spiritless, dominated, like Isabel, by Leoncio. Leoncio wants to sell all his property in the village and
never return there. He wants José María to go to live with him
in the city, as he may be heir to the family's wealth, but
José María must first be educated. José María hates his mother
and Leoncio, and harbors the intention of avenging his father's
death. In a conversation with José María, his mother, doña
Isabel, realizing that the boy is waiting for the opportunity to
confront Leoncio and kill him, confesses that his father is not
Marciana's brother as he had thought. She tells him that she
made everyone believe that he was the boy's father in order to
hide the truth which she has not and still is not able to reveal.
José María insists that she tell him who his real father is, but
she refuses. In reply, José María indignantly accuses her of
lying in order to protect her brother. The secret of the identity
of José María's real father is kept throughout the play, and is
not revealed until the final tragedy bursts forth a moment before
the curtain falls.

José María and Leoncio finally confront each other in this last
scene. Doña Isabel is present. Leoncio, wanting as always to
impose his will, insists that José María go to the city with them.
José María emphatically refuses and in the argument which follows finally insults Leoncio and his lineage. When the boy says
that he has not even forgiven his mother, Leoncio replies:

LEONCIO. You do well not to forgive her, for because of her you
are ill-born.

DOÑA ISABEL. Who are you to say it! So ill-born!

JOSÉ MARÍA. Ill-born? Because of whom? Not because of my
father. Now only his blood speaks in me to damn what I carry of
yours, of your family, your name, your lineage.

LEONCIO. And if I should slap your face?

DOÑA ISABEL. *(Stopping José María)* Silence! What are you going
to do?

José María has drawn his knife and intends to attack Leoncio,
who is also ready for the fight. Doña Isabel intervenes and in the
struggle José María is wounded in the hand with the knife,
which falls to the floor. Doña Isabel picks it up and thrusts it
into Leoncio's breast. The play ends with these words:

[125]

JOSÉ MARÍA. What have you done?

DOÑA ISABEL. You can see, I have killed!

JOSÉ MARÍA. No, you, no! I was the one to kill him; he killed my father!

DOÑA ISABEL. No; I have killed your father. This was your father.

JOSÉ MARÍA. *(Burying his face in his hands and turning away.)* God help us!

DOÑA ISABEL. Yes! God help us! God . . . Only God!

As in *The Ill-Beloved,* the whole play is built around the last scene. The real identity of José María's father is kept secret in order to take advantage of the final effect and to shatter the nerves of the spectators with the revelation of incest. This melodramatic device is too forced, too sought after, much more than in *The Ill-Beloved.* This kind of sensationalism can only please the mass audience.

The play was quite successful in Buenos Aires, where it was first performed (December 6, 1945), and later in Madrid (January 10, 1947). Yet it is a somewhat unconvincing work, as are almost all of the other plays in which Benavente abandons his characteristic style of light comedy. It is not in the rural dramas but in the satirical and psychological plays with light and not very profound themes that Benavente's artistic successes must be sought.

In this play and in *The Ill-Beloved* Benavente wanted to come close to Greek tragedy. In a self-critique published in the newspapers to advertise the première Benavente writes:

As a Greek tragedy, which is its model by intent, but from which in actuality it is quite remote, in *The Noblewoman* the seeds of tragedy have already been shown when the play begins. The audience only witnesses the consequnces. It is the "domination complex" which Adler substituted for Freud's sexual complexes which influences human behavior.[2]

Benavente's allusions to Greek tragedy and to Adler's complexes should not be taken too seriously. As for Leoncio's domination complex, if he is indeed possessed by it, it is because the author says so and because it may be implied by the other characters' remarks. His character is not shown on stage. We only witness the consequences of the drama, as the author himself

says. The center of the play is the sensational revelation of incest. The characters themselves are not sufficiently developed.

III   *The Lady of the House*

This is a rural play which is very different from the other two
discussed. Almost completely without action, it is built around
a feminine character, Dominica, who is married to Feliciano,
a peasant Don Juan. Resigned to the amorous misbehavior of
her husband who has several children by other women, she
takes heart and even seems to be proud that other women fall
in love with her husband. Everything changes radically when
she finds she is going to have a child. From an attitude of
apparent indifference to everything, she turns into a jealous
woman, she is more interested in her house and becomes an authentic "lady of the house."

In spite of the central character of Dominica, who is of a certain interest because of her silent and suffering heroism, it is
really more a play about rural customs and atmosphere than a
character play. The action is so slight that the first two acts
consist mostly of atmosphere creating scenes and character presentation. It is a good, although too extensive, portrait of the
gossip and trivialities, the misery and the greatness of the people
of any small town.

In the third act there is only one incident by which the author
intimates the possibility of tragedy. One evening Feliciano goes
on horseback to visit one of his mistresses. His brother, José,
waits in hiding for him, ready for anything, because he believes
that Feliciano is going to see José's wife, who had been in love
with Feliciano. Feliciano has an accident, falls from his horse
and hurts himself, unable to reach town. Everything turns out
for the best and the play ends with music, songs and merriment.
As in many plays, Benavente again avoids tragedy and conflict.

The play has been excessively praised by many critics. Ismael
Sánchez Estevan calls it "a masterpiece."[3] Andrés González
Blanco states that it is "the most irrefutable of his plays, [and]
constitutes a real and true success."[4] Angel Lázaro considers it,
together with *The Ill-Beloved, The Witches' Sabbath* and *The
Bonds of Interest,* "the culmination of Benavente's theater."[5]
Antonio Guardiola calls it "a play of marvelous perfection and

beauty";[6] Angel Valbuena Prat, although he lists certain objections, says that it is "perhaps superior" to *The Ill-Beloved*, and that it "is one of the author's best efforts."[7] Others have said and often repeated that it is Benavente's best play. The author himself considered it one of his favorite dramas and in the face of objections to the verisimilitude of the character of Dominica, who appears to be glad that her husband is deceiving her with other women, said: "I assure you that the woman of *The Lady of the House* is not a product of my fantasy; she is the most womanly woman in all my plays."[8]

Without denying that the character of Dominica is well designed and conceived with a certain truth and beauty, these praises, it seems to me, go too far. The work is really rather mediocre. It portrays scenes of rural life and customs with liveliness and charm, but this is not enough. These are only secondary elements in a play, and the main character, although interesting, never succeeds in filling the stage with enough force to lift the play above the second-rate.

Of the three plays included in this group, only *The Ill-Beloved* is outstanding enough to be considered alongside Benavente's masterpieces like *The Bonds of Interest* or *The Witches' Sabbath*.

The eight short dramatic pieces that Benavente wrote under the title of *Fantasy Plays* are meant to be read rather than presented on stage, although two of them have, indeed, been produced on stage: *El encanto de una hora (The Magic of an Hour)*, in the Teatro de la Princesa in Madrid, December 30, 1905; and *El criado de don Juan (Don Juan's Servant)*, in the Teatro Español of Madrid, March 29, 1911. It is the first book which Benavente published. They are eight experiments in short theater in which the author is already writing in a style very different from that of the theater of his time, a style with poetic aspirations. The theme of love, central to the first six plays, dominates. The longest is *Cuento de primavera (A Tale of Spring)* with its fourteen characters and two acts.

These eight little plays present a world of imagination and dreams, written in a language of Modernist making. Rubén Darío said of them that they "are delicate and spiritual fables strung together on a silk thread which you will find, at times, with no loss in the comparison, to be like the mental filigree of Shakespearean dialogue, the Shakespeare of *Midsummer Night's Dream* and *The Tempest*. The intuitive and clearly feminine soul of the poet creates delightful gala balls, perfumed scenes, little figures like those seen on fans and snuff boxes, taken from the milieu of the paintings of Watteau to serve as receptacles for the psychological complications and problems of life."[2] Some of his plays like *El dragón de fuego (Fire Dragon)* and *La novia de nieve (Snow Bride)* are also written in the same "precious" style.

The plays he wrote as children's theater should also be included in his minor theater. In some of them, like *El príncipe que todo lo aprendió de los libros (The Prince Who Learned Everything out of Books)*, he brings together the charm of a children's story with the mature irony of his best theater. Benavente's minor theater, in short, is an important chapter of his total production.

CHAPTER 11

Benavente and Morality

THE most widely varying opinions have been expressed on the question of the morality of Benavente's work. José Vila Selma, writing from a firm and rigid religious position as a Catholic, states that the author "completely lacks moral values."[1] He later goes on to say that "the often immoral themes, not only of Benavente's theater, but of all our contemporary literature, absorbs all literary creation."[2] Andrés González Blanco, on the contrary, says that "Benavente has always been a moralist in the theater."[3]

Benavente himself, in the face of the many contradictory statements which have been made about this aspect of his work, has repeatedly expressed his position: "I will never defend my plays as literary works, but I will defend them as works of indisputable morality. If in one of them there is something which may appear to be sinful, I am not the one who is speaking; it is some character, for whose morality I am not responsible . . . Unfortunately these evil characters are the ones who always speak most truthfully. Only God and my artistic conscience know how much one has to lie in order to moralize!"[4]

Here there is a clear contradiction: for, if in order to moralize one must lie, Benavente, in his own words, does not intend to moralize, at least in the ordinary sense of the word. There is no doubt that through those characters of doubtful morality who "speak most truthfully" the words of the author himself are expressed.

Again and again he says: "If, among many, there is one obvious defect in my works, it is that of revealing myself too much through my characters . . . If one were to extract an ideology from my plays, one would soon notice the clear line, if not of my thought—I am the first to recognize it—certainly of my feelings."[5] On another occasion:

[132]

Benavente and Morality

Sacred oratory was my first literary manifestation [he refers to the fact that in his childhood he would deliver sermons to his little friends]. For this reason, perhaps, my plays have, among others, the defect of being too sermonizing . . . My mania for pedagogy, or rather education, has also had great influence on the sermonizing nature of my plays; nothing in life has so upset me as bad manners. There is no need to say that in Spain I have been constantly perturbed. For this reason my plays are full, I might even say inundated with advice and educational maxims. This has helped neither my plays nor the education of my fellow countrymen.[6]

The advice and educational maxims which Benavente expressed through his characters and their attitude toward the crucial problems of life frequently do not conform to commonly accepted ideas of morality; that is, they are not in accord with conventional morality which is more or less associated with religious norms for behavior, norms which on the other hand everyone says he accepts but which almost no one follows. Thus Benavente says ironically that "Only a fourth of the spirit of morality, rightness, and justice which the public of the theater assumes to possess would be sufficient to make this world a paradise."[7]

Again we find the theme of hypocrisy, a theme which dominates Benavente's work: actions of experienced reality, opposed to theoretical norms of conduct expressed in beautiful words. Benavente places the individual in the world and in society, alone, isolated, and closed up within his own conscience. He never places above him, above his individual conscience, any religious, moral or ethical norm which will serve him as a guide and determine his actions. His only guide is that of his feelings and instincts. Only within himself can man seek some light in the darkness, a certain order in chaos. If he finds it, it is always inside of him, almost always in conflict with established social norms. The affirmation of his individuality, of his feelings—he seems to say—is the struggle of man as a social being. Benavente's themes are almost always based on this struggle. It is what is now called the search for identity.

Benavente seems to excuse man from any guilt in the errors and injustices he inevitably commits in his relationships with his fellow men. The words which Germán speaks to Leoncio, after violently insulting him, in *The Evil They Do Us*, can be heard through all his work: "It's true. What fault is it of yours? What fault is it of anybody's? No one is guilty; we are all unfortunate souls, we should all forgive each other . . . It's life, it's life."

Nor does Benavente look for a solution in his "areligious" view of life. He is a pessimist, and doesn't seem to expect anything good from man, from human nature. Yet his is not a tragic pessimism. It is a skeptical pessimism, often cynical and smiling: the pessimism of an indifferent spectator who merely shrugs his shoulders. He wants only to be a witness, to reflect faithfully the society of his time without pointing out any specific consequences.

He had already said in the preface to *The Noblewoman* that "life is, perhaps, the result of a blind force." This is the attitude attacked by those writers situated in a narrowly religious position. José Vila Selma states that Benavente is not a Christian writer: "I have tried, again and again, to find a concept of weakness which approaches the Christian concept and have not found it . . . Weakness . . . exists as a common denominator in the picture of life which Benavente gives us. But it is not weakness conceived from the Christian point of view, but weakness as the only possible natural moral position, without hope of betterment."[8] Elsewhere he says: "He who delves deeply into man—and not the individual being—can only be pagan."[9]

Evidently, Benavente, as he is reflected in the themes of his works, does not find a firm hold, outside of man, of man's conscience, of his inner self. His characters do not follow absolute religious or moral norms. They, as did Benavente himself, lack religious faith.

His attitude—and that of his characters—does not nevertheless cease to be human and meaningful, even moral. The proof lies in the fact that the public understood him very well; it identified with his characters, and what they say and do in his plays did not seem strange or uncommon, even to Catholics. Vila Selma, concerned about this phenomenon, offers his explanation: "If . . . Jacinto Benavente's ideology is repugnant to the righteous conscience and the meaningful view of life, why has he been so admired by the public for so long? I have found only one reason: because occultly and secretly, in his themes, he favors egoism and rebellion, because he favors self-sufficiency, because he believes in the ethical greatness of life as an end in itself."[10]. Apparently the audience who applauded him believed, essentially, in the same things as did his characters. Perhaps it is all a part of the "existentialist" mark of our age, part of contemporary sensibility.

Benavente himself confirms all that has just been said, in his view of the world and of life:

> The North Star which guided me in my directionless wandering has been the journey, with no object or final goal, which Shakespeare offers to us as the most pleasant journey ever to be undertaken. Neither religion nor philosophy has ever guided me . . . Religion! My spirit has been so religious that it could scarcely have *one* religion. One! If some flattered my imagination, none satisfied my reason. For imagination and persuasion, nothing like Buddhism, a religion for philosophers; among the philosophical doctrines, I always preferred those of the philosophers who were also artists—Plato, Plautinus, St. Augustine; and among the moderns—Schopenhauer and Nietzche . . .[11]

Nevertheless, one should never take Benavente too seriously as a moralist or as a philosopher. His is a skeptical, disillusioned spirit which seeks the truth with none of the preconceived notions accepted in the name of absolute values and with little hope of finding the truth. But he does not go far enough; he does not delve deeply enough. He remains always on the surface of problems. His attitude is more literary, intellectual and coldly rational than authentically vital; full of cleverness and insinuation rather than of profoundly vital resonances. At least, this is true as far as it can be gained from his works. He lacks forcefulness even when he writes in all seriousness. He lacks transcendence.

I *Political Ideology*

Any attempt to fit Benavente into a particular ideology in the political sphere is hopeless. One can find in his work and in his life ample evidence to support any thesis. Because of his volubility and inconsistency, one may try to fit him into different political ideologies, precisely because he didn't have any. He reacted according to the circumstances of the moment, out of convenience or out of fear, making statements which he later denied. One cannot take him seriously on political matters. Seemingly, he was extraordinarily impressionable and capricious and acted in accordance with his momentary bent.

During the Spanish Civil War (1936-1939) which he spent in the Republican Zone, he declared himself, surely out of momentary convenience, to be on the side of the Republic. In a newspaper interview which he held in Valencia, in September of 1936, he speaks of how the war caught him in Barcelona, in a hotel. After spending the first few moments of confusion and shots in the streets, during which he took refuge with other guests in the hotel basement, he was taken to a commissary for anarchist workers. He says: "They accused me of being a reactionary. I have never been. I have been and am a liberal man, perhaps of the old school, to whom violence is repugnant. But within me, as I have said, there is an author who, perhaps in spite of me, is a revolutionary. When the new order was established, I came peacefully to Valencia."

To the question "Are you anti-Fascist?," he tactfully avoided answering in saying "I have never worshipped those at the bottom nor those at the top . . . I will only say that like my two brothers I was educated in secular schools, for priests or friars never rule in my home; there were never religious images in it. No one has lashed out at the vices of the rich in his plays as I have. You have bombed them from outside their fortress; I, from within. With the pen and the word I have criticized their hypocrisy and their superficiality."[12] He goes on to say that he never sought ridiculous characters among the common people, but among the upper classes, and that he always satirized the wealthy aristocrats.

He spent the war in the Republican Zone, with no trouble. Yet he was uncomfortable. He never felt at home among the lower classes, among the proletariat. To get into the good graces of the Republic, he wrote then *Santa Rusia (Holy Russia)*, first performed on October 6, 1932. It concerns a group of emigrants, Russian revolutionaries, who lived in extreme poverty in London around 1903. Among them there appears the figure of Lenin, who in the last scene in a public park, enters on stage surrounded by children carrying a red flag on which is written: "Workers of the world, unite!" Everyone sings the *Internationale,* which can still be heard as the curtain falls. He also traveled for several months in 1929 through Russia; upon his return, when a newspaperman asked what was his greatest dream of the moment, he replied: "To go to live in Russia."

Scarcely had the Civil War ended when he made enthusiastic overtures toward Franco and on October 30, 1940, he premièred *Aves y pájaros (Birds and Other Fowl),* which he called a "Comedy in the style of Aristophanes." He now wanted to be in a good position in the "new situation" and the play has a clearly political intent. The common birds—buzzards, crows, magpies and others of that sort—are the Republicans. The noble birds—eagles, nightingales, etc.—are those allied with Franco. The little birds are in trouble, afraid, but the eagles come to liberate them. At the end of the performance, Benavente spoke to the audience and set forth cries of enthusiastic endorsement of the new political situation. The play is very bad, among the worst he ever wrote. He convinced no one with it, least of all the Falangists, who considered it an ineffective demagogic tribute.

In 1948, in three articles published in *La vanguardia (The Vanguard)* of Barcelona (January 25, February 19, and April 1), he also showed himself to be an enthusiastic supporter of Franco's politics in harshly attacking the "Reds." In the newspaper *ABC* (July 18, 1948) he calls the uprising led by Franco a "miraculous crusade."

But Benavente had flirted with all political attitudes, sometimes with those of the right and at other times with those of the left. All were only gestures and poses of the moment.

The only political stance in which he seems to have shown some consistency is in his inclination toward socialism: "Socialism has all my sympathy. I firmly believe that within a few years the civilized world will be socialist, or it won't be at all."[13] He repeated this statement on several occasions. In one article, referring exclusively to Spain, he says: "If I have faith in one political doctrine, it is in socialism, except some of its leaders;

but as I believe that socialsm is not yet capable of running Spain, meanwhile I am a Monarchist. At the moment I believe that the Monarchy is irreplaceable in Spain."[14]

There are in his plays numerous passages for which many people consider him to be a revolutionary writer. For example, in *La verdad inventada (Truth Invented)*, first performed in 1932 during the Republic, he places this little speech in the mouth of a marquis:

> Great lineages are gone; all that is past and I am not among those who want to go back, for what? Let the new people, those we have always called the lower classes, replace us; and in order that they may successfully replace us, I don't think we ought to be hostile to them, on the contrary; all that we have lost is not worth so much that we should spend our lives trying to get it back. It will be better for us to try to assure that what is new will be better, and if everyone works together in love and harmony, why shouldn't we succeed?[15]

In these plays, as in *Alfilerazos (Pin Pricks)*, produced on June 18, 1924, he attacks reactionary groups. One can also find hymns to freedom in his plays. Yet the intellectuals have always criticized Benavente's work, noting that it lacks a clear ideological system and is indifferent to social problems. Social and political problems did not interest him. Only occasionally did he make statements or write plays in which he let himself be carried away by his momentary feelings. Yet he never raises serious questions, and limits himself to censuring the hypocrisy of the upper classes. He was very pleased by flattery, and, seemingly, was more satisfied with the treatment which conservative groups accorded him. As he says: "If I received some favor from a government, it was always from the conservatives."[16] He always found himself very much at home among them, because Benavente, at heart, in his life and in his work, was a conservative.

II *Religious Ideology*

If Benavente's political position was ambiguous, his religious attitude was always quite clear. We have already made some comment on it. From what we know of his life, from what is reflected in his work and from the author's own statements, we may come to a definite conclusion: Benavente lacked religious faith. The problem of religion did not interest him. José Vila Selma has written a book, *Benavente, fin de siglo (Benavente at the Turn of the Century)*, trying to show the lack of religious values in his work. He even states that Benavente's attitude is not Christian, and comes to the following conclusion: "We must conclude that Benavente is not interested in the beyond. God does not exist in his plays."[17]

Benavente has spoken out very clearly on this subject. His play *The Evildoers of Good* was attacked as anti-clerical, and Benavente, commenting on what was being said about it, declared: "I am not a hypocrite. It seems to me that I have said quite clearly that I am not a believer . . . You know that it doesn't matter to me what may be said . . . I have always put art above all religious or political beliefs. I want art to be free of all sectarian influence."[18]

Commenting on his visit to Lourdes, he says: "I drank the miraculous water and it produced such a disturbance in my stomach that it almost forced us to delay our departure, something I would have been the first to deplore, because I didn't like Lourdes at all . . . I have a way of being incredulous, which is to be a believer in the possibility of everything. I study effects, causes don't worry me. Nothing has ever seemed to me to be of another world which can happen in this world . . ."[19]

In some of his verse, he is even irreverent:

> For all the times I made my Mother cry
> Because of what I am,
> I know that my Mother will have forgiven me.
> But have I forgiven myself? No!

> For having been born as I was born,
> As God wanted it to be,
> I know that God will have forgiven me,
> But have I forgiven God? No! [20]

As for his anti-clericalism, it is clearly expressed in the statements of some of his characters and in what he himself says. In *Para el cielo y los altares (For Heaven and Altar)*, there is a harsh attack against certain attitudes of the higher ecclesiastical hierarchies. One has only to remember the cited passage in which a Roman nuncio says of saints that "in life they are very troublesome."[21]

At times he expresses his anti-clericalism with jokes of questionable taste, as in *Truth is Suspect:*

ROMANA. This very thing: there are many children of a marriage which are the children of the husband of another marriage. The only children in my town of whose parentage we were certain were the nephews and nieces of the priest.

ALMUDENA. Woman!

ROMANA. No, my dear. I'm not saying what you think. They were really his nephews and nieces, the children of a sister, a very scrupulous and decent lady about whom nobody ever had anything to say.[22]

And in a lecture, he makes a similar reference: "The Church, always clever and with great foresight, decreed that priests should be called "Father," realizing that children, when visiting, are often imprudent."[23]

It is not necessary to cite any more cases in which Benavente shows himself clearly to be a man without religious belief and with a well-defined anti-clerical attitude.

CHAPTER 12

Benavente's Non-Dramatic Works

THE writings of Benavente which fall outside the field of drama are of interest because of their quantity and quality. The extraordinary number of theatrical works he wrote permitted him to dedicate himself only marginally to other literary efforts. Nevertheless, he published, also in great abundance, poetry, short stories, dramatic sketches meant to be read rather than produced, works of literary criticism, memoirs, a book of *Letters from Women*, lectures on many subjects and more than four hundred newspaper articles. It is thus fitting to comment briefly and generally on the diverse facets of Benavente's literary personality as revealed in these writings.

In almost all his plays, one can note a tendency toward expository prose within the dialogues. Many of the characters' dialectical speeches go beyond the strictly dramatic. For this reason the excess of "literature" in his plays has been widely criticized. But because in general the dramatic action, the plot conflict, is secondary in the majority of his plays, these long speeches in the mouths of the characters do not fit badly into the intellectualized tone of what is happening on stage.

Also as a result of this tendency, he places a "prologue" at the beginning of some of his plays which, although it goes beyond the dramatic, does help to set the tone of the action. This happens in plays like *The Witches' Sabbath, The Bonds of Interest, The Happy and Confident City, A Tale of Love,* and a few others. The prologues of *The Bonds of Interest* and of *The Witches' Sabbath* are beautiful pieces of prose which the author fuses with the spirit of the drama, even though they are situated outside the action of the play.

The first work which Benavente published, *Fantasy Plays* (1892), is a collection of eight short plays, from two to seven pages in length (with the exception of "A Tale of Spring" ("Cuento de primavera"), which extends to fifty-six pages). They are little dialogues with imaginary action, early experiments by the future playwright, more for reading than for stage production. All are written with a tendency toward "preciousness" in form, in a careful style which always attracted the author and which he used again in many of his plays. These little dramatic pieces are the middle step between his prose works and his dramas.

In 1898 he published *Figurines,* twenty short tales, some in dialogue form, which present in synthesis an idea of the author illustrated with an example. They are little works in the embryonic stage—intimations of what would follow later: the literary game-playing of a young writer who is searching for the right road. They have varied themes: the secrets which a man keeps in his brief case ("La cartera"); a conversation on the nature of art ("Among artists," "Entre artistas"); a letter from one woman to another, warning her about a Don Juan ("A Letter from a Woman," "Una carta de mujer"); a Christmas Eve party in the home of a marquise, where the guests, bored, think that they could have spent the evening better in any other place ("An Aristocratic Christmas," "Nochebuena aristocrática"); a dialogue between a princess about to be married, who dreams of impossible loves, and her friend ("Royal Wedding," "Bodas reales"); a dialogue between the daughter of some marquises and the daughter's friend, a married man, who are forced to break off their friendship in the face of other people's gossiping ("Mad Virgins," "Vírgenes locas"), etc. Some of these scenes are reminiscent of others in his later plays.

In 1905 he published *The Down of the Thistle,* a collection of eighteen stories, dialogues, and short essays on varied themes, many on love. If Modernist touches crop up in *Figurines,* the tone of *The Down of the Thistle* is often that of a rather stale, sentimental Romanticism with clear formal tendencies of the new prose of Ruben Darío. These two works must clearly be seen as a young writer's attempts to experiment with themes and style. In *The Down of the Thistle* this experimentation takes the form of very short stories: "The Storming of the Bastille" ("La toma de la Bastilla"), "The Compadre's Revenge" ("La venganza del compadre"), "Profit" ("Los réditos"), "The Wise Men" ("Los Reyes Magos"). There are also short dialogues: "A Tale of Mardi Gras" ("Cuento de Carnaval"), "Choosing A Dress" ("Elección de traje"), "Darling Daughter" ("Hija del alma"). Fairy tales appear: "Minstrel of Misery" ("Cantor de la miseria"), "The Horseman of Death" ("El caballero de la muerte"), "The Pardonable Sin" ("El pecado venial"). There are poeticisms of circus themes: "The Clowns" ("Los clowns"), "The White Elephant" ("El elefante blanco"), "The Poem of the Circus" ("El poema del circo"), etc. The themes and styles which Benavente later developed are to be found in both *Figurines* and *The Down of the Thistle*. They contain the source of what is typically Benaventine, his preferences and inclinations.

In another direct and more conversational style he wrote longer satirical stories, among which "To Skin the Cat" ("Para que el gato sea limpio"), a penetrating satire on Spanish literary life, and "A New Colloquy of the Dogs" ("Nuevo coloquio de los perros") are outstanding. In both Benavente demonstrates great mastery of the story in dialogue form.

In *Letters from Women* (1893) he already shows himself to be a penetrating observer of feminine psychology. In his time his prose signified a decisive step toward simplicity and naturalness of expression. In the familiar language of feminine correspondence he makes known the many facets and hidden aspects of the soul of woman as mother, sister, wife, sweetheart, and lover. In Benavente's later work woman is almost always the center of action and reflections of these letters can be found scattered throughout his plays.

In addition, Benavente possessed sharp critical sensibility. He expressed it in essays which generally treat literary themes, often about the theater. He developed many of them in public lectures for which he was very much sought after. These essays fill more than three hundred pages of his *Complete Works*. His ideas are clearly expressed in a direct, concise prose which is always perfectly suited to the theme. They demonstrate the fertility of his mind in commentary and analysis. Among his outstanding critical essays are "The Psychology of the Playwright" ("Psicología del autor dramático") and "Oedipus, Hamlet and Segismundo."

His most extensive prose work is that of the hundreds of newspaper articles he published, according to him, because he was tired of writing plays with a deadline. In his *Complete Works* these articles fill more than 1500 pages. They are works written in a clear, unadorned prose and directed to the educated reader, although they do not ignore the typical reader. They are grouped under the titles "Pan y letras" (among them "Popular Theater" ("Teatro popular"), "Source Material for a Play" ("El material de la obra dramática"), "Circus clowns" ("Los payasos del circo"), "The Piety of Science" ("La piedad de la ciencia"), "Summer Scenes" ("Escenas de varano"); "Acotaciones," untitled notes which discuss themes taken from news items in the daily press, on the sorrow of death, feminine clothing, the Mardi Gras, divorce, bullfighting, etc. Many are about literature. The most numerous are those published under the title "Table Talk" ("De sobremesa"). They are delightful weekly chronicles, full of wit and charm, written in a clear and noble journalistic prose. There are conversations, notes and commentaries on all subjects: the theater, politics, international affairs, *costumbrista* articles on the Madrid of his time etc. All are contemporary, and reveal Spanish life of that time. They were pleasing to the reader of his period, and today, too, can be read with great interest for their amenity and their depth of understanding of apparently trivial matters. Benavente was an excellent journalist and was awarded the Mariano de Cavia Prize, which places him among the best Spanish newspaper men of his day.

Benavente is always a good prose writer, whether in drama or in some other genre. He sometimes gets carried away with formal *préciosités*, but when he uses a simple, unadorned style, his prose is on the level of the best of his era.

CHAPTER 13

Benavente as a Poet

BENAVENTE was always a lover of poetry and a would-be poet himself. His first works, written in prose—*Fantasy Plays* (1892), *Figurines* (1898), *The Down of the Thistle* (1905) —clearly show his attempt to reach the level of poetry, in concept as well as in form. His second book, *Poems* (1893), as the title indicates, is a book of poetry. Attempts at poetic invention often appear in some of his plays, in action and dialogue alike.

Perhaps the greatest aspiration of his life was to be a poet, both within and outside of his dramatic work. When he speaks of rhythm in dialogue in his lecture "Psychology of the Playwright," he says that "dialogue without rhythm is dialogue without a soul," that our thought, like our heart, has its rhythm; that without perceiving this rhythm, "without a perfect musical— which is to say emotional—sensitivity to words, it is impossible to be a playwright, as it is impossible to be a poet. *And if one is not a poet, one cannot be a playwright.*"[1] [My italics].

In a newspaper article called "The Theater of the Poets," he advocates a poetic theater, and tries to attract poets into writing for the stage: "Poets of Spain, I, who would give all of my plays for only one of your sonnets, I say to you with all the sincerity of my love for poetry, come to the theater."[2]

There is no doubt that Benavente wanted to be a poet, and, indeed, considered himself as such. But at the same time he was well aware of his limitations. In a conversation Angel Lázaro asked him:

—Do you write verse easily?
—Yes . . . The verses in *The Bonds of Interest*, when I came to the moment in the play in which the characters recite them, I wrote with

almost the same ease with which I had been writing the prose of the dialogue.

—Why don't you write poetry?

—Because I only like good poetry—and mine isn't.[3]

He refers here to his book *Poems,* which was received by both his critics and readers alike with cool indifference. It is not surprising, for these poems lack spontaneity, originality and freshness. The effort and artifice of a writer who never succeeds in raising himself above the level of a careful versifier is all too obvious. In some of these poems—"My Muses"[4] for example—there are echoes of Bécquer filled with easy sentimentalism; in others the tone is more reminiscent of Campoamor's "humoresques." Yet their spirit is much closer to Campoamor's than to Bécquer's.

For example, his jesting skepticism appears in these "Songs":

> I deceived someone I know
> and you have deceived me;
> she had deceived someone else,
> as another will deceive you.
>
> Ah, my little friend,
> look how lucky I am!
> For when I went to embrace her,
> A pin stuck in my heart.
>
> *(Sonatas and Songs)*[5]

Benavente, it seems, had few illusions about his talent as a poet. Perhaps he was thinking of himself when he wrote:

To an Unsuccessful Poet

> Infinite hopes and limited ability,
> saddest disparity of sorrowful humanity!
> To feel poetry, and in inadequate expression
> to fall clumsily, searching for the ideal.
>
> .   .   .   .
>
> Saddest disparity of sorrowful humanity!
> Oh, to feel the desire to fly
> and in return, to have been denied strong wings.
>
> *(Poems)*[6]

Benavente never published another book of poetry, although there are some poems scattered throughout his plays. He also left many poems unpublished. In his *Complete Works* there are 116 poems which were found in manuscript form among his papers. As in *Poems*, the dominant theme is love, and the tone and quality are similar.

There is a considerable difference of opinion on the poetic quality of some of Benavente's plays. In the occasion of the opening of his Children's Theater in Madrid, December 20, 1909, the Mexican poet Amado Nervo, citing the words of a critic in *El Imparcial* seems to agree with him that Benavente, "more than a playwright, is a poet of exquisite sensibility who finds the sources of his inspiration, which other poets found in flowers, the sea or the stars, in his love for children. This is the Children's Theater which opened yesterday afternoon . . . The work of a poet, a great poet."[7]

Amado Nervo, commenting on the appeal to poets which Benavente had made two years earlier, lamented the fact that it had been forgotten, and that "few people miss poets on the boards of the stage. Nevertheless, the idea of the poetic theater continues to come into its own. In the past two years, Benavente has produced two obvious successes in *The Bonds of Interest* and *The Prince Who Learned Everything Out of Books*, two clearly poetic plays."[8]

Ruben Darío stated: "The true power of Benavente lies in the fact that he possesses the inner vision, the all-encompassing view of a poet in which he conveys the magical virtue of his secret to all he touches."[9]

Manuel Sánchez Carmargo, speaking of Benavente's theater, wrote: "Another hidden meaning of his theater is its poetic significance; but this poetic significance is so intimate, so exquisite, that it never enters into the visible structure of his dialogues, but remains almost hidden, like a distant flower which sends forth its fragrance from its hidden corner. Benavente has brought to his theater a poetry without words, so firm and so solid, that it makes itself felt only in tone."[10] Sánchez Camargo recognizes that Benavente's "poetry in verse" is not of great stature and that he never succeeded in mastering "direct" poetic expression, but he makes it quite clear that there is a poetic spirit which permeates Benavente's theater.

[147]

When we talk about poetry, as when we talk about "art," we don't know with complete assurance what we're talking about. The appreciation of poetry is something very personal, a kind of inner sensitivity mediated by many factors. The opinions cited above are worth considering, but for one reason or another, they are based on a very limited, narrow interpretation of the poetic phenomenon. They don't convince me. I see no "poetry" in Benavente's plays, especially in the formal aspect of his style. At times, in plays like *The Night of Lights, Cinderella, Snow-Bride, The Fire Dragon* or *The Gypsy Duchess,* one can see on the author's part an effort to convey a poetic "conception," a general tone which seeks to communicate to the play a "climate" or vague sense of the poetic. All in vain, in my opinion.

It seems that in these plays Benavente confuses poetry with fantasy, or sometimes with exterior decoration, as in *The Smile of Mona Lisa* and *The Princess Without a Heart,* for example; or what is even worse with a cheap sentimentality with mawkish trimmings as in *Stronger than Love, Field of Ermine,* or *The Necklace of Stars.* There is an enormous distance between what in Benavente's plays may be mistaken for poetry and the authentic poetic creation in the plays of Casona, or of Lorca, for example.

The authentic, human poetic feeling escapes Benavente when he wants to capture it in his plays. Impulses toward the poetic which arise in his plays often sound false, for here Benavente slips into unreserved fantasy or into a sticky sentimentality which borders on "corniness." The result is something stale, emotionless, artificial. What is usually confused with poetry in Benavente is something cold, dehumanized, superficial: either fantastic dreams, things about magic used symbolically or allegorically, or notes of an exaggerated sentimentality. All this filled with "pretty" words and expressions of a facile sentimentalism. It seems that Benavente lacks depth, emotion, and above all, innocence.

There is too much malice in the depths of his soul. At the end of *The Princess Without a Heart* he says: "It was a fairy tale in naive rhythms . . . the game of a poet with the soul of a child." And this is precisely what he lacks, in order to be a poet, the soul of a child. He is too reflective, cerebral, and deep down a skeptic bordering on cynicism.

Benavente's clear mind was well aware of his limitations in the art of poetry. On occasions he indicates that he wants to escape the coldness of the conceptual to lift himself to other levels and to dream freely. For example, in the prologue to *A Tale of Spring,* he says: "No reflections. We are going to dream, and the author, dreaming, invites you to do so."[11]

In "My Muses," from *Poems,* he gives us a magnificent and revealingly accurate spiritual self-portrait. It is a masterpiece of analytical introspection, full of sincerity and intuition, that shows us how well he knew himself, even though the tone of the poem is rather ambiguous. The reason for his failure as a poet is perfectly expressed in these verses:

> I do not believe in myself.
> Without faith, without spirit,
> doubt and sarcasm together
> freeze inspiration beneath my brow.
> A mixture colder and more powerful
> than that which makes an iceberg of boiling water.
>
> . . . .
>
> If the ideal lives in his poetry
> the song does not die with the poet.
> But, oh! deep within me moves
> that joking, impious little devil
> who destroys the souls wherein he lives.
> For him every ideal is but a whim,
> he lifts his disdain even unto heaven
> and scorns all, in spite of me.
> He shows insignificance beside greatness;
> if he sets foot in the temple, with great impiety
> he sees incense only as a bad odor
> and in his stubborn pride
> sees only solecisms in words of love
> and misspelled words in love letters.
>
> Shutting off the horizon before me
> he easily plays with words;
> he opens a thousand abysses
> before my uncertain step;

losing himself in the path of pursuit
the lights of the dawn of my life
he buries in the shadows of dusk.

He is entrenched in my tortured mind
and in payment of my dreams and illusions
sends back in cruel malice
the echo of his joking laughter.[12]

A marvelous self-portrait. These verses clearly reveal Benavente's authentic personality which is plainly reflected in his life
and his work. Here he appears as he is, without a mask: the
mask he wears from time to time when he wants to escape from
the "joking little devil" which never hid his true being as a
skeptic, who was often a cynic in spite of himself. He wants
to dream, to poeticize, but he cannot. These lines are a genuine
expression of his attitude toward life written at age twenty-
seven, when he still could have expected something of illusion
in his soul, and faith in the dreams and fantasies into which his
imagination fled as a refuge, in contrast to the coldness of his
soul. They explain for us, perhaps better than anything else,
the author and his work.

Notes and References

Chronology

1. All the titles may be found in the original Spanish and in translation in the Appendix, pages 165-76.

Chapter One

1. Jacinto Benavente. *Things Remembered and Forgotten: Memoirs (Recuerdos y olvidos: Memorias)* (Madrid: Aguilar, 1962). pp. 118-19.
2. *Ibid.*, p. 117.
3. *Ibid.*, p. 50.
4. *Ibid.*, pp. 53-55.
5. *Ibid.*, p. 166.
6. *Ibid.*, p. 116.
7. Jacinto Benavente. *Complete Works (Obras completas)* (Madrid: Aguilar, 1941-1958), IX, 690. Hereinafter referred to as *O.C.*
8. Ismael Sánchez Estevan. *Jacinto Benavente and His Theater (Jacinto Benavente y su teatro)*, Barcelona: Ariel, 1954, p. 35.
9. Jacinto Benavente. *Things Remembered and Forgotten*, p. 69.
10. *Ibid.*, pp. 229-31.
11. *Ibid.*, pp. 233-35.
12. *Ibid.*, pp. 423-24.
13. Federico C. Sáinz de Robles. *Jacinto Benavente* (Madrid: E. Madrileñas, 1954), pp. 8-9.
14. Angel Lázaro. *The Life and Works of Benavente (Vida y obra de Benavente)*, Madrid: A. Aguado, 1964, p. 32.
15. Benavente, *O.C.*, XI, 467.
16. *Ibid.*, p. 27.
17. *Things Remembered and Forgotten*, p. 122.
18. Sánchez Estevan, *op. cit.*, pp. 172-73.
19. *Things Remembered*, p. 26.

Chapter Two

1. Daniel Poyán Díaz. *Enrigue Gaspar: Half a Century in the Spanish Theater (Enrique Gaspar: medio siglo de teatro español)*, Madrid: Gredos, 1957, p. 342.

2. *Ibid.*, p. 11.

3. Angel Valbuena Prat. *Modern Spanish Theater (Teatro español moderno)*, Zaragoza: Partenón, 1944, p. 117.

4. Sánchez Estevan, *op. cit.*, p. 96.

5. *Loc. cit.*

6. Benavente. *O.C.*, VII, 891.

7. Benito Pérez Galdós. *Our Theater (Nuestro teatro)*, Madrid: Renacimiento, 1923, pp. 141-42.

8. *Ibid.*, p. 151.

9. José Deleito y Piñuela. *Pictures of Theatrical Madrid at the End of the Century (Estampas del Madrid teatral fin de siglo)*, Madrid: Calleja, n.d., p. 179.

10. José Vila Selma. *Benavente at the Turn of the Century (Benavente, fin de siglo)*, Madrid: Rialp, 1952, p. 240.

11. Benavente. *O.C.*, XI, 471.

12. *Ibid.*, 697-700.

13. *Ibid.*, I, 365.

14. Walter Starkie. *Jacinto Benavente* (London: Oxford U. Press, 1924), p. 211.

15. Gonzalo Torrente Ballester. *Panorama of Contemporary Spanish Literature (Panorama de la literatura española contemporánea)*, Madrid: Guadarrama, 1961, p. 192.

16. Benavente. *Theater (Teatro)*, sixth edition (Madrid: Calleja, 1929), I, 86-87.

17. Adolphe Thalasso. *The Free Theater (Le Théâtre Libre)*, Paris: Mercure de France, 1909.

18. *O.C.*, I, 62.

19. Vila Selma, *op. cit.*, p. 24.

20. José Martínez Ruíz, "Azorín." *The Generation of '98 (La generación del 98)*, Madrid: Anaya, 1961, pp. 37-38.

21. Andrés González Blanco. *Contemporary Spanish Dramatists (Los dramaturgos españoles contemporáneos)*, Valencia: Cervantes, 1917, p. 92.

22. Vila Selma, *loc. cit.*

23. Jacinto Grau. *The Prodigal Son. Pygmalion (El hijo pródigo. El señor de Pigmalión)*, Buenos Aires: Losada, 1956, p. 7.

Chapter Three

1. The so-called *Generation of 1898*, or *Generation of '98*, refers to a group of Spanish writers who gained prominence at the end of the nineteenth century and at the beginning of the twentieth century. The date which gives the generation its name is that of the war between Spain and the United States, in which Spain lost the

last remains of its extensive colonial empire. This disastrous war awakened the conscience and the sensitivity of a group of writers, who, with a keen and penetrating critical outlook, set about analyzing Spanish history and culture, while at the same time seeking new forms of artistic expression.

The term Generation of '98 was first made popular, in 1913, by one of the members of the generation, José Martínez Ruiz, better known by his pseudonym "Azorín." This harshly critical attitude toward one's own culture was not new in Spanish literature, but it was sharpened by the loss of Spain's colonies. Although the term has now become definitely established in studies of Spanish literature, there has always been much discussion about the existence of such a generation, because the differences between the writers who make up the generation are as great, if not greater, than the similarities. The many critical studies which have been published do not coincide in the writers they choose to include in this group, but the names usually associated with the Generation of '98 are: Angel Ganivet and Miguel de Unamuno, considered precursors; Pío Baroja, Antonio Machado, "Azorín," Ramón del Valle-Inclán, Juan Ramón Jiménez, Ramiro de Maeztu and Jacinto Benavente.

2. *Modernism:* A Spanish-American literary movement, whose greatest representative was the Nicaraguan poet Rubén Darío, who is considered to have initiated the movement with the publication of his works *Blue (Azul)*, 1888, and *Profane Prose (Prosas profanas)*, 1896. In addition to its Hispanic roots, there are, in Modernism, influences from the French Parnassians and Symbolists, as well as clear Romantic precedents.

Qualities generally considered characteristic of Modernism are: the search for new forms of expression; the attempt to enrich the language itself; an exaggerated concern for form, for the rhythm and musicality of words; pessimism and melancholy; the exotic nature of its themes. A movement contemporary with that of the Generation of '98, it influenced some of the writers of that generation, particularly Juan Ramón Jiménez, Valle-Inclán and Benavente. Yet, Modernism and the Generation of '98 are two different movements. Modernism is essentially a literary, poetic, or formal movement. The Generation of '98 is, rather, a critical or ideological attitude. Nevertheless, the two movements often appear as one in a single writer, or even a single work. Together they make up the reformation, the renaissance of Spanish literature at the end of the nineteenth and the beginning of the twentieth century.

3. Rafael Ferreres. *The Limits of Modernism (Los límites del modernismo)*, Madrid: Taurus, 1964, p. 41.

4. Dámaso Alonso. *Contemporary Spanish Poets (Poetas españoles contemporáneos)*, Madrid: Gredos, 1965, third edition, p. 85.

5. Gonzalo Torrente Ballester. *Contemporary Spanish Theater (Teatro español contemporáneo)*, Madrid: Guadarrama, 1957, p. 334.

6. ———. *Panorama of Contemporary Spanish Literature*, p. 191.

7. ———. *Contemporary Spanish Theater*, p. 84.

8. Domingo Pérez Minik. *Discussions on Contemporary Spanish Theater (Debates sobre el teatro español contemporáneo)*, Sta. Cruz de Tenerife: Goya, 1953, p. 114.

9. Angel Valbuena Prat. *History of the Spanish Theater (Historia del teatro español)*, Barcelona: Noguer, 1956, p. 573.

10. *Ibid.*, pp. 574-75.

11. Andrés González Blanco. *Contemporary Spanish Dramatists*, p. 49.

12. Guillermo Díaz Plaja. *Modernism and the Generation of '98 (Modernismo frente a Noventa y ocho)*, Madrid: Espasa-Calpe, 1951, p. 118.

13. *Ibid.*, p. 80.

14. "Azorín." *The Generation of '98*, p. 32.

15. José Martínez Ruíz, "Azorín." *Complete Works (Obras completas)*, Madrid: Aguilar, 1948, VIII, 882.

16. Manuel Machado. *A Year in the Theater (Un año de teatro)*, Madrid: B. Nueva, 1917, pp. 85-86.

17. Miguel de Unamuno. *Soliloquies and Conversations (Soliloquios y conversaciones)*, Buenos Aires-Mexico: Espasa-Calpe, 1947, p. 115.

18. Ricardo Baroja. "Valle-Inclán in the Cafe" ("Valle-Inclán en el café"), *The Pen (La pluma)*, IV, 32 (1923), p. 56.

19. "Azorín." *The Generation of '98*, p. 90.

20. *O.C.*, VI, 416.

21. *Ibid.*, 543.

22. *Ibid.*, 354.

23. *Ibid.*, 313-21.

24. *Ibid.*, II, 185-86.

25. *Ibid.*, VI, 477-78.

26. *Ibid.*, 503-4.

27. *Ibid.*, 551.

28. *Ibid.*, 552.

29. *Rubén Darío, Complete Works (Obras completas)*, Madrid: Mundo Latino, n.d., XIX, 79.

30. Pedro Salinas. *Spanish Literature: Twentieth Century (Literatura española: Siglo XX)*, México: Robredo, 1949, p. 24.

Notes and References

Chapter Four

1. Díaz-Plaja. Prologue to *Benavente and his Theater* by Ismael Sánchez Estevan, p. 9.
2. González-Blanco. *Contemporary Spanish Dramatists*, p. 123.
3. Pérez Minik. *Discussions on Contemporary Spanish Theater*, p. 108.
4. Sáinz de Robles. *Jacinto Benavente*, p. 23.
5. Valbuena Prat. *History of the Spanish Theater*, p. 575.
6. *O.C.*, VI, 630.

Chapter Five

1. *O.C.*, VI, 629.
2. *Things Remembered and Forgotten: Memoirs*, p. 328.
3. *Loc. cit.*
4. *O.C.*, XI, 111.
5. Vila Selma. *Benavente at the Turn of the Century*, p. 233.
6. *O.C.*, XI, 234.
7. *O.C.*, IV, 66.
8. *O.C.*, III, 1161.

Chapter Six

1. *O.C.*, VII, 80-81.
2. "Benavente and Chekhov," *The Times Literary Supplement*, London, September 18, 1924, p. 324.
3. Underhill, *Plays by Jacinto Benavente* (New York: Ch. Scribner's Sons, 1921), Introduction, p. ix.
4. "Azorín." *Complete Works*, p. 301.
5. Underhill, *op. cit.*, p. x.
6. *O.C.*, VII, 76-78.
7. Valbuena Prat. *History of Spanish Literature (Historia de la literatura española)*, Barcelona: G. Gili, 1963, seventh edition, III, 414.
8. *O.C.*, XI, 466.
9. Underhill, *op. cit.*, p. viii.
10. *O.C.*, VII, 78-79.
11. *Ibid.*, p. 83.
12. On Benavente as a poet there are some comments in Chapter 13.
13. Underhill, *op. cit.*, p. vii.
14. *O.C.*, XI, 468.
15. Alarcón. "Benavente as an interpreter of woman," *Poet Lore*, 1918, XXIX, 201-4.
16. Ismael Sánchez Estevan. *Jacinto Benavente and his Theater*, p. 77.

Chapter Nine

1. Sánchez Estevan. *Jacinto Benavente and his Theater*, p. 139.
2. *Ibid.*, p. 271.
3. *Ibid.*, p. 115.
4. González-Blanco. *Contemporary Spanish Dramatists*, p. 130.
5. Lázaro. *Life and Works of Benavente*, p. 50.
6. Guardiola. *Benavente: His Life and his Prodigious Theater* (*Benavente: Su vida y su teatro portentoso*), Madrid: Espejo, 1954, p. 102.
7. Valbuena Prat. *History of Spanish Literature*, p. 420.
8. *O.C.*, VII, 78.

Chapter Ten

1. *O.C.*, VI, 602-3.
2. Rubén Darío, *Complete Works*, p. 79.

Chapter Eleven

1. Vila Selma. *Benavente at the Turn of the Century*, p. 128.
2. *Ibid.*, p. 159.
3. González-Blanco. *Contemporary Spanish Dramatists*, p. 68.
4. *O.C.*, VII, 889.
5. *O.C.*, XI, 233-34.
6. *Things Remembered and Forgotten*, p. 66.
7. *O.C.*, VII, 625.
8. Vila Selma, *op. cit.*, p. 169.
9. *Ibid.*, p. 154.
10. *Ibid.*, p. 119.
11. *O.C.*, XI, 290-91.
12. From an article published in *El mercantil valenciano*, September 25, 1936.
13. *O.C.*, VI, 1019.
14. *O.C.*, XI, 43.
15. *O.C.*, V, 1115.
16. *Ibid.*, p. 44.
17. Vila Selma, *op. cit.*, p. 212.
18. Lázaro. *Life and Works of Benavente*, p. 54.
19. *Things Remembered and Forgotten*, pp. 395-96.
20. *O.C.*, X, 927-28.
21. *O.C.*, V, 402.
22. *O.C.*, V, 1089.
23. *O.C.*, VII, 221.

Chapter Thirteen

1. *O.C.*, VII, 79-80.
2. *O.C.*, VI, 669.

Notes and References

3. Lázaro. *Life and Works of Benavente*, p. 197.
4. *O.C.*, VI, 1033.
5. *Ibid.*, p. 1041.
6. *Ibid.*, p. 1044.
7. Amado Nervo. "Beginning of a Children's Theater" ("Inauguración del teatro para los niños"), *Language and Literature (Lengua y literatura)*, Madrid: B. Nueva, 1921, second part, p. 157.
8. *Ibid.*, p. 147.
9. Rubén Darío. *Complete Works*, XXII, 8.
10. Quoted in *Jacinto Benavente*, by Federico C. Sáinz de Robles, p. 26.
11. *O.C.*, VI, 349.
12.

No creo en mí. Sin fe, sin entusiasmo
hiela la inspiración bajo mi frente
una mezla de duda y de sarcasmo.

Mezla más frigorífica y potente
que la industrial y química, que funde
en témpano glacial le agua hirviente.

. . . .

Cuando en su canto lo ideal palpita,
muere el poeta, su canción no muere.
Mas, ¡ay!, dentro de mí tenaz se agita
un diablillo burlón, procaz, impío,
que destroza las almas donde habita.
Para él todo ideal es desvarío,
al cielo eleva su desdén intenso
y hace mofa de todo, a pesar mío.
Muestra la pequeñez junto a lo inmenso;
si el templo pisa, con fruición impía,
llama tufo al aroma del incienso
y solo advierte en su tenaz porfía,
en las frases de amor, los solecismos;
en las cartas de amor, la ortografía.
Hábil en combinar paralogismos
al cerrar horizontes a mi paso,
abre a mi paso incierto mil abismos,
y al perderse en la senda del acaso,
las luces de la aurora de mi vida
sepulta entre las sombras del ocaso.
El se posa en la mente enardecida
y en pago vil de la ilusión soñada,
repercute con saña maldecida
el eco de burlona carcajada.

Selected Bibliography

PRIMARY SOURCES

The reader may turn to the Appendix for a list of Benevente's works, arranged chronologically.

SECONDARY SOURCES

Selected books and articles, arranged alphabetically by authors' names.

ALARCÓN, MARIANO. "Benavente as an Interpreter of Woman," *Poet Lore*, XXIX, 1918, 201-5. Previously published in *Coram Populo*, Madrid, 1916. On the meaning of woman in Benavente's theater.

ALONSO, DÁMASO. *Contemporary Spanish Poets (Poetas españoles contemporáneos)*, Madrid: Gredos, 1965.

AZNAR, S. "On *The Bonds of Interest*" ("Sobre *Los intereses creados*"), *Cultura española*, February, 1908, pp. 70-77.

"BENAVENTE AND CHEKHOV." *The London Times Literary Supplement*, September 18, 1924, p. 324. An anonymous article which includes comments on four of Benavente's plays. It establishes an interesting parallel between the theater of Benavente and Chekhov.

BONILLA Y SAN MARTÍN, A. "Jacinto Benavente," *Ateneo*, Madrid, January, 1906, pp. 27-40.

BROUTA, JULIO. "Spain's Greatest Dramatist," *Drama*, November, 1915, pp. 555-67. The author places Benavente among the foremost playwrights of his time. He writes of both the man and the writer.

BUCETA, E. "On *The Bonds of Interest* ("En tonro de *Los intereses creados*"), *Hispania*, IV (1921), 211-22. Discusses the precedents of the characters of the play found elsewhere in world theater, and their relationship to Benavente's own creations.

BUENO, MANUEL. *Contemporary Spanish Theater (Teatro español contemporáneo)*, Madrid: B. Renacimiento, 1909, pp. 129-77. Very personal, penetrating comments.

Selected Bibliography

CEJADOR Y FRAUCA, JULIO. *History of Spanish Language and Litera-ture (Historia de la lengua y literatura castellana)*, Madrid: Archivos, 1919, pp. 226-61. A good study.

DARÍO, RUBÉN. "Contemporary Spain" ("España contemporánea"), in his *Complete Works (Obras completas)*, Madrid: Mundo Latino, n.d., XIX, 77-80. Articles published in *La Nación* on Spanish life at the turn of the century. Lively and charming; Darío expresses great admiration for Benavente.

DELEITO Y PIÑUELA, JOSÉ. *Pictures of Madrid Theater at the Turn of the Century (Estampas del Madrid teatral de fin de siglo)*, Madrid: Calleja, n.d., I. Clear and penetrating ideas of an his-torian who knew the theater well.

DÍAZ-PLAJA, *Guillermo*. *Modernism and the Generation of '98 (Modernismo frente a Noventa y Ocho)*, Madrid: Espasa-Calpe, 1951. A complete, thoroughly documented study of these two literary movements.

DOS PASSOS, JOHN. "Benavente's Madrid," *The Bookman*, 1921, no. 53, pp. 226-30. Reprinted in *Rosinante to the Road Again* (New York: G. H. Doran, 1922), pp. 182-95.

EGUÍA RUIZ, CONSTANCIO. "A Playwright in the Academy" ("Un dramaturgo en la Academia"), in *Literature and Literary Men (Literatura y literatos)*, Madrid, 1914, Chapter V. Contains a good evaluation of *The Bonds of Interest*.

FERRERES, RAFAEL. *The Limits of Modernism (Los límites del mod-ernismo)*, Madrid: Taurus, 1964. A collection of essays. The first two form an accurate delineation of Modernism and the Generation of '98.

GÓMEZ DE BAQUERO, E. Articles in *La España moderna*. On *The Evildoers of Good:* January, 1906, pp. 160-66; on *The Bonds of Interest:* January, 1908, pp. 169-77.

GONZÁLEZ BLANCO, ANDRÉS. *Contemporary Spanish Dramatists (Los dramaturgos españoles contemporáneos)*, Valencia: Cervantes, 1917, pp. 27-168. Considers Benavente one of the world's great dramatists.

GONZÁLEZ RUIZ, NICOLÁS. *Spanish Literature (La literatura es-pañola)*, Madrid: Pegaso, 1954, pp. 19-30.

GUARDÍOLA, ANTONIO. *Benavente: His Life and Prodigious Theater (Benavente, Su vida y su teatro portentoso)*, Madrid; Espejo, 1954. An impassioned defense of Benavente's theater.

JAMESON, STORM. *Modern Drama in Europe* (London: Collins, 1920), pp. 239-45. An excellent commentary on Benavente's theater.

[159]

JESCHKE, HANS. *The Generation of 1898 (La generación de 1898)*, Madrid; E. Nacional, 1954. Defends the existence of the generation its origins, character, stylistic theories, etc.

LÁZARO, ANGEL. *Life and Works of Benavente (Vida y obra de Benavente)*, Madrid; A. Aguado, 1964. Interesting facts about Benavente's life, and a prologue by Benavente himself.

MACHADO, MANUEL. *A Year of Theater (Un año de teatro)*, Madrid: B. Nueva, 1917. Articles published previously in *El Liberal*. Immediate impressions of plays presented in Madrid: *Well-known People*, pp. 81-88; *The Evil They Do Us*, pp. 200-208. Information about the effect Benavente's plays had on theater audiences of that time.

MALLO, JERÓNIMO. "The Theatrical Production of Jacinto Benavente since 1920" ("La producción teatral de Jacinto Benavente desde 1920"), *Hispania*, XXXIV (February, 1951), 21-29). The author believes that the quality of Benavente's theater declines after 1920.

MARTÍNEZ RUIZ, JOSÉ ("AZORÍN"). *The Generation of '98 (La Generación del 98)*, Madrid: Anaya, 1961. Selected writings of Azorín on the generation of '98, edited by Angel Cruz Rueda. Shows the ideas about the generation of one of its most characteristic representatives.

MUÑOZ, MATILDE. *History of Spanish Dramatic Theater (Historia del teatro dramático español)*, Madrid: Tesoro, 1948. An overall picture of Spanish drama from its beginnings.

NERVO, AMADO. "Beginning of Children's Theater" ("Inauguración del teatro para niños") in *Language and Literature* (Madrid: B. Nueva, 1921), second part, pp. 163-71. Also on Benavente, "Poetic Theater" ("El teatro poético"), pp. 138-50.

ONÍS, FEDERICO DE. *Jacinto Benavente* (New York: I. Españas, 1923). A brief study—41 pages—on the significance of Benavente's theater at that time.

PÉREZ DE AYALA, RAMÓN. *The Masks (Las máscaras)*, Buenos Aires; Espasa-Calpe, 1944. A harsh and unjust judgment of Benavente, generally derogatory and too personal. Also includes studies on other writers (Galdós, Valle-Inclán, Linares Rivas, etc.).

PÉREZ GALDÓS, BENITO. *Our Theater (Nuestro Teatro)*, Madrid: Renacimiento, 1923. Articles with different dates, interesting in their point of view of Spanish theater at the end of the nineteenth century.

Selected Bibliography

PÉREZ MINIK, DOMINGO. *Discussions on Contemporary Spanish Theater (Debates sobre el teatro español contemporáneo)*, Sta Cruz de Tenerife; Goya, 1953. A polemic volume which nevertheless contains some deep intuitions about Spanish and European theater. The major portion of the book was written before 1936.

POYÁN DÍAZ, DANIEL. *Enrique Gaspar—A Half-Century in the Spanish Theater (Enrique Gaspar—Medio siglo de teatro español)*, Madrid; Gredos, 1957. The most complete study of the theater of Gaspar, one of Benavente's predecessors.

RIVAS CHERIF, C. "The Works of Benavente in the light of the Nobel Prize" ("La obra de Benavente al fulgor del premio Nobel"), *La Pluma*, (Madrid, 1922), III, 433-41.

SÁINZ DE ROBLES, FEDERICO CARLOS. *Jacinto Benavente* (Madrid: E. Mádrileños, 1954). A brief study—43 pages—with information of biographical interest.

SALINAS, PEDRO. *Spanish Literature: Twentieth Century (Literatura española: siglo XX)*, México; Robredo, 1949. The first part, on the Generation of '98 and Modernism, is of interest.

SÁNCHEZ ESTEVAN, ISMAEL. *Jacinto Benavente and His Theater (Jacinto Benavente y su teatro)*, Barcelona: Ariel, 1954. A biographical and critical study, with detailed commentary on Benavente's plays, artists and theaters. Sánchez Estevan's attitude is clearly reactionary, and he unsuccessfully tried to fit Benavente into it.

STARKIE, WALTER. *Jacinto Benavente* (London: Oxford U. Press, 1924). A good study which shows great critical sensitivity. A discussion of many of Benavente's plays in detail, and Benavente's relations to the European theater as a whole.

TORRENTE BALLESTER, GONZALO. *Panorama of Contemporary Spanish Literature (Panorama de la literatura española contemporánea)*, Madrid: Guadarrama, 1961, pp. 191-96. Points out the limitations of Benevente's theater.

——. *Contemporary Spanish Theater (Teatro español contemporáneo)*, Madrid: Guadarrama, 1957. There are references to Benavente in several chapters, especially in "Benavente and Society" ("Benavente y lo social"), pp. 65-71.

UNDERHILL, JOHN GARRET. "Benavente as a Modern," *Poet Lore*, XXIX (1918), 194-200. Penetrating comments on *The Governor's Wife* and *The Witches' Sabbath*.

——. *Plays by Jacinto Benavente*, First Series, New York: (Charles Scribner's Sons, 1921). Contains an interesting introduction to the translation of *His Widow's Husband, The Bonds of Interest, The Evildoers of Good* and *The Passion Flower (The Ill-Beloved).*

————. *Plays by Jacinto Benavente,* Second Series, (New York: Charles Scribner's Sons, 1921). Contains an excellent preliminary study plus translations of the plays *No Smoking, Princess Bebé, The Governor's Wife* and *Autumnal Roses.*

————. "The Modern Spanish Drama", *Drama League Monthly,* 1917, no. 6, pp. 562-64. A very good study on Benavente plus interesting comments on several of his plays.

VALBUENA PRAT, ANGEL. *History of the Spanish Theater (Historia del teatro español),* Barcelona: Noguer, 1956, pp. 573-88. An interesting evaluation of Benavente's theater.

————. *History of Spanish Literature (Historia de la literatura española),* Barcelona: Gili, 1963, seventh edition.

————. *Modern Spanish Theater (Teatro moderno español),* Zaragoza; Partenón, 1944. An important general study.

VALERA, JUAN. *Echoes from Argentina (Ecos argentinos),* Buenos Aires: Emecé, 1943. Articles published in Argentine newspapers on Spanish literature. Interesting commentary on *Well-Known People,* pp. 28-31.

VIQUEIRA, JOSÉ MARÍA. *Benavente's Characters Speak (Así piensan los personajes de Benavente),* Madrid: Aguilar, 1958. An anthology of passages from Benavente's plays.

VILA SELMA, JOSÉ. *Benavente at the Turn of the Century (Benavente, fin de siglo),* Madrid: Rialp, 1952. Vila Selma wants to deny the importance of Benavente's theater because he considers it outside of the Christian concept of life. His point of view is narrow and debatable.

YXART, JOSÉ. *Dramatic Art in Spain (El arte escénico en España),* Barcelona: Vanguardia, 1894. Begins in the eighteenth century with Moratín and ends with Galdós at the end of the nineteenth century. A very personal view of writers, literary epochs and movements, with comments on the historical background and on foreign influences.

Appendix

PLAYS AND OTHER WORKS BY JACINTO BENAVENTE

Plays

(In chronological order according to the date of their première.
When the city is not mentioned, the première took place in Madrid.)

1. *The Intruder (El nido ajeno);* three acts; October 6, 1894. An excellent psychological study of love.
2. *Well-Known People (Gente conocida);* four acts; October 21, 1896. Critical satire of high society in Madrid. Very good.
3. *Mrs. Téllez' Husband (El marido de la Téllez);* one act; February 13, 1897. A satirical look at the life of artists of the theater.
4. *Light Mourning (De alivio),* February 27, 1897. A monologue written expressly for the actress Carmen Cobeña. A charming satire on social customs, in this case a widow's mourning.
5. *Don Juan;* five acts; November 30, 1897. A translation of the play of the same name by Molière.
6. *Web of Lies (La farándula);* two acts; November 30, 1897. A satire on political life in a Spanish province.
7. *Food for Wild Beasts (La comida de las fieras);* three acts and one scene; November 7, 1898. A satire on the aristocratic and wealthy upper class of Madrid. Good.
8. *Plays about Women (Teatro feminista);* one act, with music by Pablo Barbero; December 28, 1898. An insignificant little comedy.
9. *A Tale of Love (Cuento de amor);* three acts and a prologue; March 11, 1899. An adaptation of Shakespeare's *Twelfth Night.*
10. *A Surgical Operation (Operación quirúrgica);* one act; May 4, 1899. The love affairs of a married woman separated from her husband.
11. *Cruel Good-by (Despedida cruel);* one act; December 7, 1899. A satire on married love.
12. *The Angora Cat (La gata de Angora);* four acts; March 31, 1900. A good satire on high society in Madrid, its fickleness

and amorality; concerns the love affair of a painter and an aristocratic lady.

13. *An Apprentice's Journey (Viaie de instrucción);* one act and four scenes; April 6, 1900. A musical comedy with music by Amadeo Vives. A comic farce, all in fun.

14. *Through the Wound (Por la herida);* one act; Barcelona, July 15, 1900. Satire on the lack of morals in matters of love in upper-class Madrid.

15. *Style (Modas);* one act; January 15, 1901. A light satire in a comic vein. Characters of all kinds parade through a dress shop. Good.

16. *The Thing to Do (Lo cursi);* three acts; January 19, 1901. Satire on Madrid society.

17. *Unintentionally (Sin querer);* one act; March 31, 1901. A psychological comedy sketch, vaguely romantic in tone.

18. *Sacrifices (Sacrificios);* three acts; Barcelona, July 19, 1901. A psychological play about love between artists and people with money.

19. *The Governor's Wife (La gobernadora);* three acts; October 8, 1901. Ironic satire on life and politics in the provinces. The character of the governor's wife is drawn with effective psychological touches. Good.

20. *Cousin Román (El primo Román);* three acts; Zaragoza, November 12, 1901. Light satire on provincial politics, together with cynical comments on love.

21. *In Love with Love (Amor de amar);* two acts; February 24, 1902. A very good satire on love and frivolous feminine coquetry. Set in eighteenth-century France.

22. *Freedom! (¡Libertad!):* three acts; March 17, 1902. A translation of the play in Catalán by Santiago Rusiñol.

23. *The Train for Married Men (El tren de los maridos);* two acts; April 18, 1902. Light comedy.

24. *The Soul Triumphant (Alma triunfante);* three acts; December 2, 1902. Family conflicts in a middle-class atmosphere.

25. *The Automobile (El automóvil);* two acts; December 19, 1902. A comedy of the slapstick variety.

26. *The Witches' Sabbath (La noche del sábado);* called by its author "a dramatic novel in five acts"; March 17, 1903. A combination of satire, fantasy and ideas. Deals with princes, aristocrats and artists at an international summer resort. One of Benavente's masterpieces.

27. *The Favorites (Los favoritos);* one act; Seville, March 20, 1903. Based on an episode from Shakespeare's *Much Ado About Nothing.*

28. *Little man (El hombrecito);* three acts; March 28, 1903. Satire on high society in Madrid. Very good.
29. *Why is Love? (Por qué se ama);* one act; October 26, 1903. A psychological play about love in the upper middle class of Madrid.
30. *Mademoiselle de Belle Isle,* five acts; Valladolid, October 29, 1903. A translation of the play by Alexander Dumas, père.
31. *As It Really Is (Al natural);* two acts; November 20, 1903. A satirical comedy about the wealthy and aristocratic. The first act in Madrid, the second in a village. Good.
32. *The House of Good Fortune (La casa de la dicha);* one act; Barcelona, December 9, 1903. Comedy about the lower middle class of Madrid.
33. *No Smoking (No fumadores);* one act; March 3, 1904. A theatrical joke.
34. *Richelieu;* five acts; Mexico City, March 15, 1904. A translation of the play by Sir Bulwer-Lytton.
35. *Fire Dragon (El dragón de fuego);* three acts and an epilogue; March 15, 1904. A fantasy play more novelistic than dramatic.
36. *Autumnal Roses (Rosas de otoño);* three acts; April 13, 1905. Play about a rich family in which the wife saves the family with her sacrifice in spite of the philandering of her husband. Good.
37. *An Immoral Tale (Cuento Immoral);* one brief scene; July 22, 1905. Comic monologue.
38. *The Countess' Fright (El susto de la Condesa);* one act; November 15, 1905. A joke with dialogue.
39. *Manon Lescaut;* seven scenes; November 30, 1905. A Romantic and fantastic love story. Written in collaboration with Alfonso Danvila.
40. *The Evildoers of Good (Los malhechores del bien);* two acts; December 1, 1905. A satire on the hypocrisy of distinguished ladies of a small town who engage in works of charity and wreak more evil than good. Excellent.
41. *The Understudy (La sobresalienta);* one act; December 23, 1905. A lyric farce with music by Ruperto Chapí.
42. *The Cicada-Ants (Las cigarras hormigas);* three acts; December 24, 1905. A comedy, for entertainment only.
43. *The Magic of an Hour (El encanto de una hora);* one act; December 30, 1905. First little play of *Fantasy Plays (Teatro fantástico).* A dialogue between two porcelain figures.
44. *A Good Marriage (Buena boda);* three acts; performed in several high society parties in 1905. Based on the play *Un Beau Marriage* by Emilio Augier.

45. *Stronger Than Love (Más fuerte que el amor);* four acts; February 22, 1906. A rather sentimental play about love among aristocrats, with touches of crude cynicism.
46. *Princess Bebé (La princesa Bebé);* four acts; March 31, 1906. Benavente called it "scenes from modern life." A satire on human ideals and aspirations, with a wealth of ideas. Characters include kings, princes, nobles and commoners. Excellent.
47. *Who's Afraid of Love! (El amor asusta);* one act; February 8, 1907. A comedy set among the aristocratic and the wealthy.
48. *The Owls (Los buhos);* three acts; February 8, 1907. On the loneliness of two intellectual old bachelors.
49. *Grandmother and Granddaughter (Abuela y nieta);* one act; February 21, 1907. Inconsequential dialogue between a Marquess and her granddaughter.
50. *The Enchanted Cup (La copa encantada);* one act; March 16, 1907. A musical comedy based on a story by Ariosto; music by Vicente Lleó.
51. *We Are All One (Todos somos unos);* one act; September 21, 1907. A comic farce with music by Vincente Lleó.
52. *The Story of Othello (La historia de Otelo);* one act; October 11, 1907. Dramatic sketch of life in the upper class.
53. *The Eyes of the Dead (Los ojos de los muertos);* three acts; November 7, 1907. A rather melodramatic tale of impossible love. Characters are middle class.
54. *The Bonds of Interest (Los intereses creados);* two acts and prologue; December 9, 1907. Moral and philosophical satire in the style of the Italian *commedia dell'arte.* Considered the author's best work.
55. *The Princess Without a Heart (La princesa sin corazón);* one act. Never performed. A fairy tale, with poetic pretensions.
56. *The Smile of Mona Lisa (La sonrisa de la Gioconda);* one act. Never performed. A fantasy with dialogue.
57. *The Lady of the House (Señora ama);* three acts; February 22, 1908. A play with a rural setting; some people consider it one of Benavente's best plays.
58. *For Small Reasons (De pequeñas causas);* one act; March 14, 1908. A satirical look at woman's domination of the family. Good.
59. *His Widow's Husband (El marido de su viuda);* one act; October 19, 1908. A very clever comedy with masterfully written dialogue. Very good.
60. *Brute Force (La fuerza bruta);* one act; November 10, 1908. A rather sentimental play about love among circus people.

61. *Toward the Truth (Hacia la verdad);* three scenes; January 20, 1909. A play examining the customs of both the rich and the poor in Madrid.
62. *Among the Clouds (Por las nubes);* two acts; January 20, 1909. About the customs of the lower middle class.
63. *Up Close (De cerca);* one act; April 10, 1909. A play about the rich and the poor.
64. *The Last Minuet (El último minué);* one act; October 23, 1909. A dramatic sketch about the courage of aristocrats facing death.
65. *The Young Lady Is Bored (La señorita se aburre);* one act; December 1, 1909. A play about love, based on a poem by Tennyson.
66. *The School for Princesses (La escuela de las princesas);* three acts; December 14, 1909. A psychological play about love, set in the place of an imaginary kingdom. An excellent study of feminine psychology. Very good.
67. *The Prince Who Learned Everything from Books (El príncipe que todo lo aprendió de los libros);* two acts; December 20, 1909. A fantasy play for children.
68. *To Earn a Living (Ganarse la vida);* one act; December 20, 1909. For children.
69. *What Can a Man Do! (A ver qué hace un hombre);* one act three scenes. Never performed. A play about social problems among the poor.
70. *The Grandson (El nietecito);* one act; January 27, 1910. Based on a story by the Brothers Grimm.
71. *Don Juan's Servant (El criado de Don Juan);* one act; March 29, 1911. The third play in his collection of *Fantasy Plays.*
72. *The Grave of Dreams (La losa de los sueños);* two acts; November 9, 1911. A play about the poor of Madrid.
73. *King Lear (El rey Lear);* A translation in prose of Shakespear's play. Never performed.
74. *In Madrid (En este Madrid);* one scene; April 2, 1913. A monologue.
75. *A Gentleman Who Renounced the World (Un señor que renunció al mundo);* one act. Never performed.
76. *The Ill-Beloved (La malquerida);* three acts; December 12, 1913. Rural tragedy. One of Benavente's masterpieces.
77. *Destiny Calls (El destino manda);* two acts; March 25, 1914. A translation of the play by Paul Hervieu.
78. *Necklace of Stars (El collar de estrellas);* four acts; March 4, 1915. A sentimental play about people who were once wealthy.

79. *Self-Esteem (La propia estimación);* three acts; December 22, 1915. A rather sentimental play about the impossible loves of business people. Good.

80. *The Truth (La verdad);* one act; published in 1915. (Not presented until January 6, 1942.) Excellent psychological dialogue on "truth," sincerity, hypocrisy. Very good.

81. *Field of Ermine (Campo de armiño);* three acts; February 14, 1916. A sentimental play about aristocrats.

82. *The Yellow Tunic (La túnica amarilla);* three acts; April 22, 1916. A translation of the Chinese legend written by George G. Hazelton and Harry Benrimo.

83. *The Happy, Confident City (La cuidad alegre y confiada);* three acts and a prologue; May 19, 1916. The sequel to *The Bonds of Interest.* Very inferior to the first play.

84. *The Evil They Do Us (El mal que nos hacen);* three acts; March 23, 1917. A psychological thesis play about love. Good.

85. *The Cubs (Los cachorros);* three acts; March 8, 1918. A sentimental play with a circus setting.

86. *Mephistopheles (Mefistófela);* three acts; April 29, 1918. An operetta with music by Prudencio Muñoz. A comedy, solely for entertainment.

87. *The Immaculate Lady of Sorrows (La Inmaculada de los dolores);* five scenes; April 30, 1918. Benavente calls it "a novel in dramatic form." A *costumbrista* play about the provincial aristocracy and the middle class.

88. *The Children's Law (La ley de los hijos);* three acts December 23, 1918. A play about a middle-class family of Madrid.

89. *Charity (Caridad);* a monologue written expressly for Rosario Pino. Not published until 1918, but presented in 1911.

90. *Loyal to All—A Traitor to All (Por ser con todos leal, ser para todos traidor);* three acts; March 6, 1919. An historical play set in a Spanish colony at the beginning of the nineteenth century.

91. *The Vestal Virgin of the West (La vestal de occidente);* four acts; March 29, 1919. An historical play about the English court at the end of the sixteenth century.

92. *Honor among Men (La honra de los hombres);* two acts; May 2, 1919. A play on the theme of honor among men. Good.

93. *The Bold One (El audaz);* five acts; December 6, 1919. An adaptation of the novel of the same name by Galdós.

94. *Cinderella (La cenicienta);* three acts and a prologue; December 20, 1919. Dramatization of the well-known tale. Good.

95. *And Now a Story . . . (Y va de cuento . . .);* four acts and a prologue; December 22, 1919. A fairy tale for children.
96. *Brute Force (La fuerza bruta);* two acts; performed in 1919. A musical comedy with music by Federico Chaves.
97. *A Lady (Una señora);* three acts; January 2, 1920. "A novel" in dramatic form, of bankrupt rich people and the ingratitude of their friends.
98. *A Woman of the Poor (Una pobre mujer);* three acts; April 3, 1920. A play about the poor of Madrid and the indifference of the wealthy.
99. *Beyond Death (Mas allá de la muerte);* three acts; Buenos Aires, August, 1922. A play about spiritualism.
100. *Why John Quit Drinking (Por qué se quitó Juan de la bebida);* one scene; Montevideo, August 30, 1922. A rather sentimental monologue.
101. *Lessons on Love (Lecciones de amor);* three acts; April 2, 1924. A simple but well-done psychological play with an upper middle-class background. Very good.
102. *A Pair of Boots (Un par de botas);* one act; May 25, 1924. A humorous play about poor people.
103. *Pin Pricks (Alfilerazos);* three acts; June 18, 1924. A satire on the pettiness of life in society. Good.
104. *Another Kind of Honor (La otra honra);* three acts; September 19, 1924. A very modern comedy of manners about the infidelity of a woman forgiven by her husband. Good.
105. *Virtue Is Suspect (La virtud sospechosa);* three acts; October 20, 1924. A light satire on the customs of the aristocracy.
106. *No One Knows What He Wants, or The Dancer and the Laborer (Nadie sabe lo que quiere, o El bailarín y el trabajador);* three acts; March 14, 1925. A light, charming comedy. Good.
107. *The Suicide of Lucerito (El suicidio de Lucerito);* one act; July 17, 1925. A satirical play on the life of actors in Madrid.
108. *The New Sons-in-law (Los nuevos yernos);* three acts; October 1925. A light satire on the business world of the rich and the aristocratic.
109. *Do You Think I Like It? (!Si creerás que es por mi gusto!);* "A dialogue in half an act"; performed in 1925. A psychological examination of the infidelity of a lady "who leads a very free life." Good.
110. *The Butterfly Who Flew Over the Sea (La mariposa que voló sobre el mar);* three acts; September 22, 1926. A play about frustrated love, set in a cosmopolitan atmosphere among the the wealthy and their parasites.

111. *Polichinela's Son (El hijo de Polichinela);* three acts and a prologue; April 16, 1927. A play about family entanglements.
112. *A Night of Lights (Una noche iluminada);* three acts; December 22, 1927. A play of magic and fantasy.
113. *At the Gates of Heaven (A las puertas del cielo);* one act; never performed. A half-serious, half-joking conversation between St. Peter and a "good soul." A real gem within its genre.
114. *The Devil Was Once an Angel (El demonio fue antes ángel);* three acts; February 18, 1928. A psychological play about love. Excellent.
115. *I Don't Want To! I Don't Want To! (!No quiero! !No quiero!);* three acts; March 10, 1928. A *costumbrista* play set among the wealthy and the aristocratic.
116. *Pepa Doncel;* three acts; November 21, 1928. A psychological play about women among aristocrats and social climbers. Very good.
117. *For Heaven and Altar (Para el cielo y los altares);* three acts and an epilogue. Never performed. Religious satire. Good.
118. *Crossed Lives (Vidas cruzadas);* "a cinedrama in two parts and an epilogue"; March 30, 1929. An attempt at a new technique showing influence of the movies.
119. *Man's Best Friends (Los amigos del hombre);* four scenes; November 3, 1930. A comedy about bulls and bullfighters.
120. *Rags of the Royal Purple (Los andrajos de la púpura);* five acts; November 6, 1930. A play about success and failure in the theater.
121. *From a Very Good Family (De muy buena familia);* three acts; March 11, 1931. A play about the difficulty of communication within a family.
122. *Literature (Literatura);* three acts; April 4, 1931. A satire on literary life.
123. *A Jazz-Band Melody (La melodía del Jazz-band);* three acts and a prologue; October 30, 1931. A play about the kindness of a "bad" woman.
124. *When the Children of Eve Are Not the Children of Adam, (Cuando los hijos de Eva son los hijos de Adán);* three acts; November 5, 1931. A play about the amorality of people without homeland or religion, lost in the world.
125. *Holy Russia (Santa Rusia);* six scenes; October 6, 1932. About Russian revolutionaries exiled in London around 1923.
126. *The Gypsy (La duquesa gitana);* five acts; October 28, 1932. A fantasy play.

127. *The Moral of Divorce (La moral del divorcio);* "a lecture in dialogue form, divided in three parts"; November 4, 1932. A delightfully funny and clever comedy.
128. *Truth Invented (La verdad inventada);* three acts; October 27, 1933. A play about family conflicts among the upper middle class and a few aristocrats.
129. *His Wife's Rival (El rival de su mujer);* three acts; Buenos Aires, 1933. A very subtle psychological study of love and friendship.
130. *Bread Eaten From the Hand (El pan comido en la mano);* three acts; January 12, 1934. A play about feminine psychology in marriage.
131. *Nor Love nor Sea (Ni al amor ni al mar);* four acts and an epilogue; January 19, 1934. A play about love in the upper middle class.
132. *Memoirs of a Citizen of Madrid (Memorias de un madrileño);* five scenes; November 8, 1934. A play about middle-class life in Madrid.
133. *The Snow-Bride (La novia de nieve);* three acts and a prologue; November 20, 1934. A very good play of fantasy and humor.
134. *Such Things Are Not to be Played with (No juguéis con esas cosas);* three acts; January 18, 1935. A play about modern life in Madrid.
135. *Anyone Knows That (Cualaquiera lo sabe);* three acts; February 13, 1935. A clever comedy with excellent dialogue. Very good.
136. *The Unbelievable (Lo increíble);* three acts; October 25, 1940. A *costumbrista* play about the gossiping of people, set among the provincial upper middle class.
137. *Birds of a Feather (Aves y pájaros);* "a comedy in the style of Aristophanes, in two parts"; October 30, 1940. A symbolic allegorical play with political overtones.
138. *Grandfather and Grandson (Abuelo y nieto);* one act; San Sebastián, August 29, 1941. A dialogue about politics.
139. *And It Was Bitter . . . (Y amargaba . . .);* three acts; November 19, 1941. A social satire on life in Madrid.
140. *The Last Letter (La última carta);* three acts; December 9, 1941. A comedy about love among royalty.
141. *Behind Closed Doors (La honradez de la cerradura);* three acts; April 4, 1942. A psychological, ethical play on the inconsistency of human honesty. Very good.
142. *It's Your Fault! (La culpa es tuya);* three acts; San Sebastián, August, 1942. A light comedy. Very good in its genre.

143. *After All, a Woman (Al fin, mujer);* three acts; San Sebastián, September 13, 1942. A play about the power of feminine will; set among aristocrats and artists.

144. *Darling Daughter (!Hija del alma!);* one act; September 17, 1942.

145. *The Lady in Mourning (La enlutada);* three acts; Zaragoza, October 16, 1942. A play about family conflicts, set in a small town, among the upper middle class.

146. *The Devil of the Theater (El demonio del teatro);* three acts; October 18, 1942. A satire on theater people.

147. *Children Lost in the Forest (Los niños perdidos en la selva),* "a dramatic novel in four chapters"; San Sebastián, January 4, 1944. A novelistic play about love among the rich.

148. *Magín the Magician (Don Magín el de las magias);* three acts; Barcelona, March 16, 1944. A theatrical comedy with an ingenious plot.

149. *An Image of Greatness (Espejo de grandes);* "an historical portrait in one act"; October 12, 1944. A delicate satire on the magnificence of the Spanish court of the sixteenth century Good.

150. *Snow in May (Nieve en mayo);* "a dramatic poem in four acts"; January 19, 1945. A psychological play about love. Very good.

151. *The Sorrowful City (La ciudad doliente);* three acts; April 14, 1945. A psychological study of sick people with "complexes."

152. *Titania;* three acts, September 25, 1945. A psychological study about love in marriage.

153. *The Noblewoman (La Infanzona);* three acts; Buenos Aires, December 6, 1945. An excellent play on the delicate theme of incest.

154. *At the Service of her Imperial Majesty (Al servicio de su Majestad Imperial);* one act; never performed. A play about the love affairs of Catherine of Russia.

155. *Abdication (Abdicación);* three acts; March 27, 1948. A rather satirical play about the aristocracy in the modern world.

156. *Divorce of the Soul (Divorcio de almas);* three acts; September 30, 1948. A psychological study of love and marriage.

157. *Adoration (Adoración);* two acts and a prologue; December 3, 1948. A play about hate and unconfessed love in an upper middle-class family.

158. *Love Must Be Sent to School (Al amor hay que mandarle al colegio);* "a comedieta in four episodes"; September 29, 1950.

A play about married couples who do not understand each other and want to separate.

159. *His Loving Wife (Su amante esposa);* "a *comedieta* in three episodes"; October 20, 1950. A play love outside of marriage among the upper middle class.

160. *You, Once and the Devil, Ten (Tú, una vez y el diablo, diez);* three acts and three interludes; Valladolid; October 23, 1950. A play about humanization through love.

161. *Mater Imperatrix;* three acts; Barcelona, November 29, 1950. A play about a mother's sacrifice for her son, set in a cosmopolitan atmosphere among people with money. Good.

162. *Life in Verse (La vida en verso);* three acts, the last divided into two scenes; November 9, 1951. A play about love among theater people.

163. *Don Juan Has Arrived (Ha llegado don Juan);* two acts and a prologue; Barcelona, April 12, 1952. A play about feminine psychology when confronted with a Don Juan.

164. *The Hound of Heaven (El lebrel del cielo);* three acts; April 25, 1952. A play about love, sin, and holiness, inspired by Francis Thompson's mystical poem *The Hound of Heaven.*

165. *To Serve (Servir);* three acts and an interlude; January 22, 1953. A fantasy with an upper-class setting.

166. *Needles in the Mouth (El alfiler en la boca);* three acts; February 13, 1953. A psychological play on the theme of love. Very good.

167. *Imprisoned Souls (Almas prisioneras);* two acts and a prologue; February 26, 1953. A play about the love affair of a mother with her daughter's fiancé. Set in chivalresque atmosphere of New World Spain.

168. *Red Riding Hood Frightens the Wolf (Caperucita asusta al lobo);* three acts and a prologue; September 23, 1953. A charming light comedy. Very good.

169. *The Sons Are as Fathers (Hijos, padres de sus padres);* two acts and an epilogue; February 11, 1954. A play about the children of an upper middle-class family of Madrid who take the initiative.

170. *A Husband in Bronze (El marido de bronce);* three acts; April 23, 1954. A satire on provincial life.

171. *To Save His Love (Por salvar su amor);* three acts and an interlude; November 2, 1954. A play about mixed-up love affairs among friends. Set in an atmosphere among the wealthy.

172. *Hamlet's Fool (El bufón de Hamlet);* three acts and an epilogue; performed after Benavente's death.

Other Works

Fantasy Plays (Teatro fantástico) (Madrid: T. Franco-Española, 1892).

Poems (Versos) (Madrid: T. Franco-Española, 1893).

Letters from Women (Cartas de mujeres), first series. (Madrid: T. Franco-Española, 1893). Second and third series, (two volumes), (Madrid: I. Marzo, 1901-1902).

Figurines (Figulinas) (Madrid: T. Franco-Española, 1898).

The Down of the Thistle (Vilanos) (Madrid: I. Fortanet, 1905).

The Theater of the People (Teatro del pueblo) (Madrid: Fernando Fe, 1909). Miscellaneous articles.

Table Talk (De sobremesa), six series, (Madrid: Ed. Hernando, 1910-1916).

Notes (Acotaciones) (Madrid: Gráficas Mateu, 1914).

Chronicles and Dialogues (Crónicas y diálogos) (Valencia: I. Pallarés, 1916).

Lectures (Conferencias) (Madrid: E. Hernando, 1924).

Things Remembered and Forgotten: Memoirs (Recuerdos y olvidos: Memorias) (Madrid: Aguilar, 1962).

In *Complete Works (Obras completas)* (Madrid: Aguilar, 1941-1958), there are many articles, lectures, letters, works of literary criticism and short stories published by Benavente throughout his life in different periodicals.

Index

Index